_____

Books by Pierre Berton

The Smug Minority

The Smug Minority

PIERRE BERTON

1969

Doubleday & Company, Inc.
Garden City, New York

11-7-90

Originally published in Canada by
McClelland and Stewart Limited
25 Hollinger Road
Toronto 16, Canada

The publishing history of *The Smug Minority* in Canada is almost as remarkable as that of its predecessor, *The Comfortable Pew*. The books are different, of course: One dealt with the hierarchy within the institution of the church. The other deals with the hierarchy within the institution of society itself. But the reactions to them have been remarkably similar.

Both books were greeted with torrents of abuse as well as wild hosannas on publication. Both caused such widespread controversy and discussion that the titles, in each case, have passed into the Canadian vernacular. (I was intrigued to notice recently that an air pollution expert had referred to Torontonians as members of "the smog minority.") And both books made publishing history in Canada.

My Canadian publisher, after reading the manuscript of the present book, made an immediate decision to break with precedent and launch it with a first printing of 100,000 books. Nothing like this had ever been attempted in a country whose English-speaking population scarcely exceeds 15 million—it is as if an American publisher decided on a first printing of one and one-half million books. Few first printings in Canada exceed 5000. Even *The Comfortable Pew*, which ultimately sold well over 100,000, breaking all sales records, was launched with a first printing of 16,000.

In the matter of magazine rights, the publisher also broke with Canadian tradition. He held an auction and offered excerpts to the highest bidder. *Two* national magazines ended up carrying excerpts from the book, paying the highest prices yet offered serially in Canada.

As I write this, the book has been in print for ten weeks and has sold about 80,000 copies. It seems likely to go into other printings. It is intriguing to note that it is selling best in places where books aren't normally purchased—in cigar stores, airports, hotel lobbies and small towns. It is, in short, being bought by people who don't normally enter bookstores and who are, in no sense, members of the literary establishment, let alone the financial one.

Immediately on publication (and even before it) the book touched off an emotional storm. It has been, perhaps, the most widely publicized book in Canada since *The Comfortable Pew*. The book critics have reviewed it at great length and in some cases have re-reviewed it. Business writers and political pundits have written columns about it. Letters to the editor have appeared in Canadian dailies attacking or defending it (or attacking and defending its critics). The country appears to be split down the middle on the subject of *The Smug Minority*. Half the comments have been embarrassingly effusive; the other half as vicious as I've ever seen in print.

Even when they worked for the same paper the critics couldn't agree among themselves. On the Calgary *Herald's* book page, Jamie Portman dismissed it all as "windy rhetoric and innuendo." On the same page, the financial editor of all people called it my "crowning achievement . . . a brilliant critique on contemporary social ethics and values." The Toronto *Telegram's* political columnist, Douglas Fisher, wrote that "this is a wonderful book" and went on to say that "there's no other recent book that compares favorably with The Smug Minority." But on the book page of the same newspaper, John Curran, in a stinging review, dismissed the whole thing as "a collection of outmoded left-wing ideas." On the Vancouver *Sun*, one writer in a full-length column, urged everyone to read the book; another, in a full-page article, said it wasn't worth reading.

The business writers couldn't agree among themselves about the book. In an apoplectic review, the editor of *The Financial Times* wrote that "there is really nothing to beat the smugness of a bleeding heart when he goes on a rampage against the cruelty of society." On the other hand, the financial editor of the Toronto *Star*, Canada's biggest paper, devoted a column to defending the book and attacking its critics.

The spectacle of the critics attacking each other was an enjoyable one. One review was even titled: *Smug Reviewers, Good Book*. And one editorial writer actually changed his mind about the book. He reviewed the first half one week and published a mocking review, then announced the following week that he'd finished the book and liked it.

Was the book well or badly researched? Political science professor Richard J. Powers, writing in the Victoria *Times*, said it was: "The book is replete with examples and case histories gleaned from many diverse sources." Across the gulf in Vancouver, the *Province's* reviewer, Lorne Parton, disagreed "[The book] is weakened by his tendency to conjecture without any research to support it."

Was the book well written or badly written? The *Financial Times* said that I wrote "like a retarded teenager." The United Church *Observer* said I communicated superbly. The Edmonton *Journal* said my style was graceless. *The Presbyterian Record* said my style was delightful. And so it went. I noticed, generally, that those who agreed with the book thought my style was brilliant; those who disagreed thought it dreadful.

Does the book say anything new? The Ottawa *Citizen* wrote that "Berton's challenge provokes fresh thinking"; but the Winnipeg *Free Press* dismissed it with the words: "We've heard it all from taxi drivers." A columnist in British Columbia declared that "twenty years ago this book would never have been written, let alone published." Another, in Toronto, insisted the book was "almost exactly thirty years out of date."

Will the book be effective? Some said it wasn't radical enough; others that it was too radical. One writer, in Edmonton, said he was infuriated because the book *didn't* make him mad. Robert Fulford, in the Toronto *Star*, on the other hand, wrote that "Berton writes with an intensity that may (and should) leave his readers burning." He said the book made *him* mad—for the right reasons. *Monday Morning*, a magazine for teachers, disagreed; it felt the book had "a complacent air where we should expect anger." On the other hand *The Presbyterian Record* said the book was "a shattering blow to complacency", and *The Prairie Messenger*, a Roman Catholic publication, said the book was "bristling with challenges to the Christian conscience." But in the Toronto *Telegram*, John Curran wrote that "to expect the general public to get indignant about this kind of stuff in 1968 is just too much." (In Ontario, one Liberal member of parliament was indignant enough to attack me in a major speech in the Legislature which made the front pages. He called me, among other things, a "phoney" and a "flatulent blatherer.")

As Robert Fulford remarked, in a witty column which discussed the reactions to the book, "*The Smug Minority* is the kind of book that brings out the best or worst in book reviewers—the worst, in most cases."

Jack MacArthur, in the same paper (the Toronto *Star*), wrote that "the critics and the columnists should be arguing about injustice. Instead they're arguing about Berton." Certainly in a good many cases, the reviewers devoted as much space to reviewing *me* as to reviewing the book. It was impossible for many of them to separate my public personality as a TV interviewer and panelist and as a radio commentator, from the views expressed between these covers. How can a man who appears to work so hard deliver a polemic against work? (This is discussed at some length in the book but many critics seem not to have read that section.) How dare a man write about poverty when he is himself financially secure? How can an apparent capitalist espouse the cause of socialism? The curious idea that only the poor can be radical appears to be widespread among newspapermen.

There was, as well, a distinct undercurrent of feeling, especially from the academic critics, that it was somehow distasteful and cheap for a popular television personality to engage in a book of social criticism. The academic reviews were remarkably grudging. It wasn't that they disagreed with what I had to say; it was just that they seemed to resent my taking ideas that had been held by a scholarly coterie and presenting them to a large public.

A typical comment came from *The Canadian Forum*, a respected monthly with a left-wing viewpoint:

"The book's essential flaw (and no doubt the reason for its mass readability) is its lengthiness. Berton takes many . . . pages to expand upon what may be considered a basic paragraph of 'our side's' thought . . . At the moment it cannot be denied that he has reached an audience this magazine never reaches."

The *Forum*, bless its heart, has yet to make a dent in the structure of Canadian society and it never will as long as it is edited for a tiny clique of professors who cannot get it into their heads that some things have to be said more than once to be effective.

The most widespread critical comment about the book was that "it contains nothing new." It seems to have infuriated the critics that most of the contents of this book has been said before by someone, sometime, somewhere, someplace. Exactly the same reaction greeted *The Comfortable Pew* on its appearance. The bishops and theologians claimed that everything I'd said in that book was well known to them. If so, one wonders, why didn't they tell their congregations?

If indeed, *The Smug Minority* is old stuff, then why all the fuss? Why is the book being bought in quantity? Why are all the magazines outbidding each other for it? Why is it causing such lengthy and emotional critiques?

There are some problems, new or not, that need to be reemphasized and restated and that is one purpose of *The Smug Minority*. Many reviewers noted, for example, that there was nothing new about poverty in Canada. ("Berton has decided to tell us his discovery that poverty exists"—Portman, Calgary *Herald*.) This ho-hum attitude tells us something about the smugness of middle-class Canadian society in 1968. The scandal is not just that poverty exists but that so many responsible people are able publicly to say "So what?" and get away with it.

In truth, most books contain "nothing new." All books of this kind are built on the work of others and future books, I hope and expect, will be built on this one. I would not plead that the present work is more than a compilation of information culled from various sources, arranged into a certain pattern and laced with opinions that the author has held for some time—as have others before him. Book reviewers, of course, have read everything and so to them nothing is new. Academics have written everything of consequence and really reem to believe that everyone else has read all of it. Only one critic in Canada, Robert Fulford, took the trouble to point out that the problem, in the case of *The Smug Minority*, was a question of audience.

"Berton is shooting at one audience—the barely literate middle class of Canada—and his critics, for the most part, will be talking about another. Unlike almost everyone else who writes about social questions in this country, Berton wants to speak not to a community but to the nation: not to a few thousand people but to hundreds of thousands."

The attitudes of the smug minority, detailed in this book, aren't new either. But they are still with us, as I discovered when the reviews appeared. A good many of my critics felt that these attitudes were outmoded and not worth attacking. ("His targets are fat and slow moving.") But many more mirrored and upheld them when they discussed the book in print. ("Every solution he proposes is based on further government control of our lives" . . . "it is no myth that he who works hard will rise". . .)

Shortly after publication it became clear to me that the most controversial section of the book was that which deals with work and leisure. Arguments on open line radio shows in which I took part confirmed me in the belief that the myth of hard work is one of the most persistent in our society. Nothing seems to cause more fury than the suggestion that some "work" would be better eliminated and that those who perform it would be better off doing something else—even if that something else constitutes an activity we don't normally define as "work." My own attempts to distinguish between "work" and "toil" and to venture the hope that some toil would sooner or later be eliminated often caused confusion and irritation as the following editorial from an Ontario newspaper indicates:

"Pierre, one of the hardest-working types in the country, appears to feel that work is wrong, somehow, degrading and absolutely unnecessary. That's the theme of the book. People should never have to feel it is necessary to work, the government should hand them a minimum amount of money to fill their basic needs. Then, if they want to work they can, but if they don't want to they should be able to lie around and do what they want to do. Sounds good, huh? . . .

"On Sunday evening, we watched members of Bowmanville's fine fire brigade spend nearly three hours risking their necks on ladders, with dense smoke pouring in their faces at a house blaze on Bradshaw St. All of them were wet, cold and dirty. According to Pierre's thinking this would be degrading work that should be eliminated. Maybe he'd have let the house burn down, possibly with everybody in it, so somebody could build another one, if and when they felt like it . . . or would that be degrading work, too?

". . . From our point of view, possibly as one of the Smug Majority, (the book) is way out in Utopia that makes Hippieland seem almost normal."

There is no point in repeating here what appears in the body of the book, but I hope it will be clear to those who read further that the editorial writer missed my point entirely. My attitudes about work and leisure may be old ones, as some of the critics have said, but it's quite clear that they are disturbingly new to large numbers of people who haven't read Weber or De Grazia.

How about Americans? This is a very Canadian book, supported largely by Canadian research. Do the smug attitudes dissected here stop at the international border?

I think not. In Canada we read most of the American columnists and most of the American magazines; and, God knows, we have every major U.S. television program and comic strip thrust upon us. It seems to me that the myths I am describing here are just as much Americans myths as they are Canadian—perhaps more so. It may be that the myths began south of the border and were imported by Canadians, along with Coca-Cola, Chevvy cars, Charlie Brown and Perry Mason. Certainly all the clichés about freedom, work, education and welfare spring glibly to the mouths of American after-dinner speakers. If anything, the U.S. counterparts of our big business associations are even more reactionary than the C.M.A. or the Canadian Chamber of Commerce.

I do not want to pretend too much for this book. It is not the first of its kind; I hope it will not be the last. Perhaps it will be a useful backstop for those who need to bolster arguments and support points of view. I do not expect that it will change society but I hope that in a few instances, at least, it will change one or two attitudes as it has in Canada. If, en route, some clichés are discarded and some well-worn and outdated words (such as "handouts") are buried forever then I will be well satisfied.

PIERRE BERTON

Kleinburg, Ontario
April 28, 1968

CONTENTS

. . . A race that binds

Its body in chains and calls them Liberty,

And calls each fresh link Progress.

Robert Buchanan

The Smug Minority

CONVERSATION FOR
THE TWENTY-FIRST CENTURY

*What was it like in the olden days, Pop? I mean around the 1960's.
. . . Was it like they show it on the TV?*

Well, now, son – you know TV tends to glamourize history out of
all recognition, sometimes. Things weren't all that good, you
know, back then.

*Gee, Pop, when you look at shows like "Tycoon" or "Astronaut" or
"Freeway Pirate," well, I mean it's pretty exciting.*

Sure, it *looks* exciting and even attractive. You see those campy,
hand-operated "cars," as they called them, meandering down the
old freeways and those strange rows of telephone poles and the
cute little "homes" with the old-fashioned patios and you get a
big kick out of it. But the people themselves led pretty dreadful
lives by our standards.

Then why do they always talk about "the good old days," Pop?

People tend to view the past through a fog of nostalgia, son. You
know – lovers spooning in the quaint drive-ins and whole families
sitting around the bar-b-q. But don't forget that for most people
life was composed of equal parts of boredom and drudgery. It was,
in essence, a serf society run by a smug minority of well-entrenched
overseers.

*Gee, Pop, that sounds like the Middle Ages. Were those people
really like serfs?*

They would have resisted the name; but in our terms they were.
In spite of the old adventures they dredge up for "Freeway
Pirate," historical evidence makes it clear that the masses of the
people who lived in Canada in the Sixties were chained to tedious
and degrading jobs which they despised; that between one-fifth
and one-third of them were prisoners of a poverty so grinding we

can scarcely contemplate it; and that only the wealthy had the freedom to enjoy a proper education.

And this smug minority you mention that ran things . . . who were they, Pop?

A small, in-bred, establishment of business and political leaders who had a vested interest in maintaining the *status quo*.

But gosh, Pop, why didn't the people revolt if conditions were as bad as all that?

Because the minority convinced the majority that life was wonderful.

Oh, come on, Pop. That's stupid.

Read your history books. You'll find that's what happened. Of course the big establishment had the help of the minor establishments – religious, educational, journalistic, judiciary – in this brainwashing.

You mean they convinced people that serfdom was an okay thing?

Oh, quite easily. The most menial and wretched toil was held to be highly honourable. It conveyed a magical thing called "status." People preferred it to happiness.

But all that poverty, Pop. Surely they didn't prefer that*? Wasn't there any kind of public planning to prevent that?*

No – quite the contrary, son. The minority convinced the majority that public planning was bad for them. They called it "government interference." They said the people would lose their hard-won freedom if they had it.

But hold it, Pop. They didn't have any freedom*!*

That's right. But the minority boasted so loudly about this non-existent freedom that they convinced the majority they had more of it than any people in history.

Gosh, Pop. I mean those people must've been real dumb to swallow that line.

Well, of course, by our standards they were wretchedly educated. The majority didn't even finish highschool. The universities, such as they were, were reserved for the privileged classes. You see they didn't pay you to get an education in those days, son. *You* paid *them*! The minority saw to that.

Pop, I just don't understand why the people didn't complain.

Because the minority convinced them that it was better that way – that anything else would be foolishly extravagant besides being an invasion of freedom.

This minority you talk about, Pop: they must have been a real bunch of hypocrites to fool the people that way.

Not at all, son. All the available evidence shows that they honestly and sincerely believed all those things themselves. You see that's what made the minority so smug.

ONE

The tyranny of a dying ethic

The Puritan hated bear-baiting,

not because it gave pain to the bear,

but because it gave pleasure to the spectators.

Thomas Babington Macaulay

1. *Is Gordon Sinclair*
    a Puritan?

My friend and colleague, Gordon Sinclair, and I were driving down the Okanagan Valley from Kelowna to Penticton on one of those cloudless August days when everything in the world seems right. As usual, we were arguing the point that everything in the world seemed wrong.

"I just don't understand you," Gordon was saying. "How can you be so totally inconsistent? How can you hold the ideas you do when you yourself have made it in spades? Yet here you are claiming you want people to pay higher and higher taxes! You're the hardest worker I know and yet you believe that people who don't work ought to get government handouts. Now you're telling me you want all the drones to go to college."

"I even want to *pay* some people to go to college," I told him. "Not just for a few years, but in some cases maybe forever."

I thought Gordon would explode. "You want to pay people not to work?" he cried. "You want to subsidize laziness? All the things you worked for – everything that's yours by right – you want to give that away?"

I started to say that I really didn't want to "give" anything away but that I was prepared to invest to a greater degree in the human product of a country which, heretofore, had done most of its investing in mines and wheatfields, oil-wells and power plants, forests and oceans – in things you can see and feel; but not in the human spirit.

But it was a hot day and I was tired and lazy, too, and all I said was that I was probably going to write a book about the subject, which he could read sometime if I ever finished it. I thought that would end the discussion but it didn't. Gordon grew more and more heated as he talked. He kept on that day and that night and for many months later when we met, as we do fortnightly, in the CBC's Studio Four on Yonge Street. I have never

seen Gordon Sinclair as worked up since the days when we used
to argue about the fluoridation of public water supplies. In this
continuing debate I have seen him grow physically angry – not
personally angry at me, for we continue to like and respect one
another – but angry at an idea. It is more than anger; it is honest
bewilderment. Gordon's fury springs out of a terrible frustration:
all his life he has worked hard and brilliantly to build a personal
fortune of which he is very proud. In his view, it is his and no one
else's, to do with what he likes. Nobody has the right to take any
portion of it from him. While other people were lying around
doing nothing, he was slaving away; now along comes somebody
who seems to advocate that the grasshoppers enjoy the fruits of
the ant's labour. Or that is the way he sees it.

At income-tax time, Gordon is particularly violent. Each year
the tax bite grows larger, and it is useless to try to point out to him
that, taxes or no taxes, his take-home pay is really more than he
can spend. Like most of us in the communications field, his
income derives from several sources, but he has figured out that
the sum he is paid as a radio commentator and newscaster is equal
to the sum he pays in tax. In his terms this means he is working in
radio for nothing. A system that allows this to happen is, to him,
something close to dictatorship.

"We've got to stop people like you!" he once cried out at me.
"One of these days a real, right-wing party is going to rally around
a leader, and we're going to call a halt to all these handouts to the
drones of this world." During the Progressive Conservative convention in September, 1967, Gordon publicly applauded the stand
of Senator Wallace McCutcheon who is opposed to further taxes
to extend the welfare state. Yet in other ways, Gordon is not a
right winger at all; his reputation is that of an iconoclast, not a
member of the establishment.

If Gordon Sinclair were some kind of a nut with no power, no
voice, and no credentials, it would be simple to forget about him.
But he is not a man easily dismissed. He is a poor boy with a
limited education who made it big, by society's standards, through
his own brains, his own sweat, and no more luck than the next
man. He broadcasts twice each day on the largest radio station in
Canada, and he commands the largest audience on that radio

station. Some people damn him and some adore him but all, including me, listen to him with mingled delight and irritation.

He did not arrive at his position by accident. He has a knack of putting his finger on the frustrations and furies of the public. There is no argument about his power: his opponents credit him with delaying by several years the fluoridation of Toronto's water supply. If he reflects the unexpressed opinions of large numbers of people, he also helps to mould and sustain those opinions.

Any faithful listener to Gordon's radio broadcasts will know that he uses several epithets. One is "do-gooder"; another is "bleeding heart"; a third is "prophet of gloom and doom." Gordon doesn't see anything gloomy about the country. As for the do-gooders and the bleeding hearts, it is clear that he considers them to be meddlers. Gordon is an individualist and he always has been. It is his strength and, to a considerable extent, the secret of his success. He stands on his own two feet, secure in the knowledge that he pulled himself up by his own bootstraps, and he doesn't want anybody meddling with his life or telling him what's good for him.

To Gordon the making of money is an honourable calling. I do not mean he works solely for money; I suspect-he would do what he is doing whether he was paid or not. But he is proud of the fact that he is one of the highest-paid members of his profession. He is frank about his income and curious about that of others, as any television viewer knows. The first words he ever spoke to me, when I met him in 1948, were: "You're talking to the only news-paperman in Canada with $100,000 in the bank." He is an investor, not a speculator. He doesn't touch his capital. He follows the market closely and is depressed when it drops, even though his losses are merely paper ones. His considerable personal charities are to him a private matter and he doesn't talk about them.

Work is as important to Gordon as money, though it is neces-sary to emphasize that the work he does is of a kind he thoroughly enjoys. He talks a good deal about work. He is angered at the idea that large numbers of people who "work" are apparently being forced to support an increasing number of people who "don't work." He has publicly referred to such people as "drones"; in his view a goodly number of them are spongers on the real workers.

He believes that many are being coddled by government handouts. For example, I have heard him talk, only half-facetiously, about "room service" and other luxuries in publicly subsidized housing developments.

He believes that if people haven't saved enough to keep them in their old age, it is generally their own fault; after all, he has done this and he didn't have a head start in life. He believes that any poor boy with guts and drive can get ahead and put himself through school. This is why he is opposed to free university education; again, he thinks that those who do all the work would be subsidizing lazy kids. For similar reasons he was personally angered when the city of Toronto paid for large numbers of school-children to visit Expo '67. Gordon thought they or their parents were quite capable of paying their own way.

These are Puritan attitudes, and while it is strange to think of Gordon Sinclair as a Puritan, it is clear that even he cannot free himself entirely from the ethic in which he was raised. His blood and his background are Scots, and he was brought up as a strict Methodist who went to church twice and sometimes thrice each Sunday by a mother who clung tenaciously to the Protestant work ethic. She was the greatest influence in his life, and of her he has written:

"Mother had a fierce, driving ambition to acquire money, because in her time, even more than now, money spelled power and security. There was no such thing as a baby bonus, old-age cheque, or unemployment benefit but there certainly were rainy days, and if you could not pay the rent, out you went. Without a job you were really in trouble."

Gordon has freed himself of many of the trappings of Puritanism; the temperance movement which Bessie Sinclair supported so fervently, along with the church itself, has aroused his scorn; but the subtler values are still there. He was raised in a world that bears very little relation to our own; he was ten years old before there was a telephone in his house and twelve before his family had electric lights. In those turn-of-the-century days, conditions must often have been appalling but in his autobiography, Gordon looks back upon them with considerable nostalgia: the German bands in the park; the itinerant evangelists on the streetcorner;

the Uncle Tom shows in the opera house; the Goat signs each spring proclaiming bock beer in the saloons; steamboat vacation trips; fishing in the Don for suckers; tobogganing at Riverdale Park; and the parade of horses on Dominion Day. These were the "good old days" before the supersonic age with its superhighways, supermarkets, and supercities, when almost everybody lived in a detached house (as the Sinclairs did) and the family unit included a vast number of aunts and uncles as well as grandparents. In this world there was a literal Hell and a Heaven with a set of pearly gates, and it is significant that to this day when Gordon Sinclair attacks religion it is the Old Time Religion he is after with its three-decker universe and its white-bearded deity.

2. *The thing we think is standing still is moving*

The general attitude that Gordon Sinclair expresses with such force and colour is one of several attitudes prevailing in Canada today; and since it is the attitude predominantly expressed by the power structure, it is a very potent one. It was analyzed at the turn of the century by the German sociologist, Max Weber, in his famous treatise on *The Protestant Ethic and the Spirit of Capitalism*. The establishment in Canada – business, judicial, educational, religious, and journalistic – still pays lip service to this ethic or to portions of it. It is obvious that the ethic is dying as the country emerges from its pioneer and Puritan past; perhaps that is why since World War II, the older generation has clung so tenaciously and so vociferously to shreds of it.

In Weber's classic analysis, it was Calvinism and later other forms of ascetic Protestantism (such as Pietism, Methodism, and some sections of the Baptist movement) that gave a religious significance to and a moral justification for worldly activity. The

Calvinist was a lonely man in the sight of God; no other individual could help him; his destiny was decreed for him in advance. To create the conviction of his own salvation – to rid himself of the overburdening fear of damnation – the Calvinist dedicated himself to labour in the Lord's vineyards. He worked industriously at his "calling" (i.e., the appointed task to which the Lord had called him) in the confident belief that he was one of the Chosen, fulfilling the duties imposed upon him by his position in the world, planning his life methodically and rationally in accordance with God's will. The Calvinist proved his faith by worldly activity, but in this worldliness he remained as ascetic as some of the Catholic monks of the Middle Ages. There was about him a hard frugality. Wealth was seen only as a symbol for a job well done, and its enjoyment, along with such other sins as idleness and the temptations of the flesh, was seen as a distraction from the pursuit of the religious life. Sex was for procreation only, and the Calvinist prescription for sexual temptations, as it was for almost everything else, was to "work hard at your calling." Cleanliness, needless to say, was next to godliness.

Thus hard work and the accumulation of money came to have for the Puritans a religious significance. Rest and leisure belonged to the next world. People who lay abed mornings were made to feel almost as guilty as those who enjoyed sex; in both cases they were losing time from their calling – to labour for the glory of God. "Wasting time" was therefore the deadliest of sins because the Puritan knew that life was short and every moment precious. Sociability, luxury, idle talk, too much sleep, inactive contemplation – all these things took time from work and were anathema. "Time is money" was not a Calvinist phrase but it sprang from the Calvinist ethic.

As we know, the Puritan rejected the joy of living, and this attitude has had its effect on Canada right to the present moment. The theatre was obnoxious to the Puritan as was all form of ostentation. The arts do not flourish in a Puritan society which, subscribing as it does to a rigid code of conduct, rejecting personal decoration, insisting upon a methodical system in life, vastly preferring steady employment to casual labour, conspires against the non-conforming artist. Such things as sidewalk cafes, love-ins, gourmet food, coffee houses, psychedelic drugs, and go-go dancers are at war with the Puritan attitude.

It is important to note, as Weber did, that the Protestant attitude towards work as a calling was unknown during the Middle Ages, when leisure time was held in greater regard than material wealth and when the accumulation of more money than a man needed was considered the lowest form of avarice. This approach to life continued to be held in the Catholic countries of Europe which did not succumb to the Reformation and helps to explain why people take two and a half hours for lunch in Paris or Vienna and only half an hour in Toronto, and why immigrants from Europe often feel themselves to be totally at odds with the atmosphere in Protestant Canada. Weber began his investigations into the ethic as a result of his observation that the overwhelming proportion of business and industrial leaders in Germany were Protestants rather than Catholics. Exactly the same has been true of French Canada. The humanist education of Quebec's classical colleges has never fitted their graduates to be captains of industry (or even *want* to be). Surely there is irony in the spectacle of French Canada embracing the work ethic of its English-speaking neighbours just at that point in time when it seems about to become meaningless!

The Puritan at his best was tough-minded, sturdy, creative, rigid – qualities that stood him in good stead in the great age of exploration which coincided with the Protestant Reformation. In a period of geographical outburst, Puritanism can be seen as a positive force, vigorous and creative. In a time when swamps have to be drained, forests hacked down, cabins erected, crops harvested, and natives repulsed, there is nothing like a group of single-minded and industrious men. In the days when there was still a physical frontier, the Puritan ethic made sense: work was necessary, slackers were indeed sinners, worldly pleasures got in the way of progress. It is interesting to note that while the present-day Puritans tend to look back with nostalgia on a vanished past, the forefathers whom they worship were forward-looking men, willing to postpone leisure, sex, joy, and freedom in the interests of future generations, and able to plant trees under whose shade they would never sit.

Of necessity, the Puritan family was a closed unit in its attitude to scarcity. It had to depend on its own resources. This attitude was reinforced by the Canadian situation where in pioneer days there was real scarcity and food had to be stored up in jars and root cellars against the long winters. The family looked after its own: the feeble-minded brother, the prodigal son, the unmarried sister, the aged and infirm grandparents. Within these family confines there was great charity and great tolerance. But this kind of family has vanished in the urban Canada of the Sixties as have the frontiers themselves.

Today it is possible to view the survivors of Puritanism as frustrated frontiersmen. Because their perception is frustrated and the frontiers, apparently, non-existent, they are, in the words of an enlightened Presbyterian minister I know, "demonically dangerous." There is a blindness here to the new frontiers. One hears again and again the wistful call for a return to "traditional values" and the nostalgic murmurings about our pioneer forefathers who lived in a world where everything had its place, where life was ordered by an established and unvarying code of conduct, where the all-embracing family provided the anchor of security and every man was on his own in the sight of God. This is the kind of world – exciting, harsh, demanding, fulfilling – for which the Barry Goldwaters, the Ronald Reagans, and the Wallace McCutcheons yearn. But it is a world that no longer exists. The sustaining institutions – family, church, and school – no longer control morals or conduct: the first has shrunk to molecular proportions, the second has lost its power to terrify, the third has been diluted and superseded by more attractive and effective media. There is no single ethic today but a multitude of ethics, and so we are experiencing the same kind of shock that Galileo's generation must have sustained when he said, in effect: "The thing we think is standing still is moving."

Today such shock waves roll over us at ever-increasing speeds. Our culture refuses to stay in one place and the artists have sensed the chaos. We continue to grope for new codes and new securities, unable to perceive that change has now become the norm and that, to survive at all, the truly modern man must be prepared to accept the repeated rabbit punches of continuous acceleration. Technological progress is changing the way we think, act, and reason, not just from decade to decade but almost from year to year. The birth control pill and television are perhaps the two most obvious examples: it is conceivable that the first may render the family unit obsolete and that the second may shatter the old concept of rational, linear thought.

Based on our present knowledge and technological ability, we can consider a whole range of future possibilities. (These are not predictions because they are with us already in one form or another.) Some of them are attractive, some repellent, but all of them are perfectly feasible.

* *Political parties may be obsolete.* There may be no need for political parties since, with highly sophisticated information systems, it will be possible to have instant referendums on specific issues rather than elect parties, as we do now, on broad principles.

* *Work, as we know it now, may be obsolete.* Two per cent of the population will be able to produce enough for everybody to eat and wear. Most of the population will be engaged in creative work or in handicrafts. There will be a much larger proportion of writers, poets, painters, and musicians to the population. As in Aristotle's time, almost everybody will play a musical instrument.

* *Language may be universal.* The computers can force the issue. When mathematicians develop a computer language, it will become mandatory for all students to learn it so that the machines can function at the sound of the human voice. People will begin to talk to each other in the same way. Those who still write in the old tongues can reach a universal audience through instant translation.

* *Libraries, art galleries, theatres, and shops may be unknown.* Books, pictures, entertainment, and goods will become available at the press of a button. If you want to learn something, a computer can scan the knowledge of the world and type out a compendium of information on the subject. Closed circuit TV will tell you what's available and list the prices. The order

will be prepared and delivered automatically. Balanced meals will be prepared at central kitchens, frozen, stored, and delivered on call. Warehouses, tin cans, and home stoves will thus be rendered obsolete.

* *Sex will be free but procreation may be controlled.* Everybody will enjoy sex freely but reproductive organs will be blocked at birth and released only if permission to reproduce is given. People will live to the capacity of their sensual natures. The number of children allowed to be born may be governed by computer forecasts and interpretations based on the present number of people, their health, and long-range climactic factors. Population figures will be projected for a hundred-and-twenty-year cycle which will be the average life expectancy. The family will become obsolete as children become part of the public sector.

* *Cash may be unknown.* Computers can tell exactly how much one earns and saves. With growing abundance and diminishing population, there'll be no need to relate human productivity to earnings. A certain amount of buying power will be credited to each man's account annually. A man's worth and status won't be equated with what he makes but with what he is. Honour will go to those whose work achieves scientific breakthroughs or pleases the senses. Some people will stay at school most of their lives. Unions, capital, private property – all these may become obsolete.

It is a pleasant pastime, this little game of science-fiction, and we could continue to play at it for several more pages. But this is enough to suggest what the possibilities are. No one has yet come within a mile of predicting the future; one can only delineate that which is feasible. Of one thing, though, we can be certain: the future will not be like the past. That is truer today than it has ever been. We cannot expect to find solutions to the New Age by looking nostalgically back to the days of our forefathers. We must find them, as they did, by casting our eyes ahead.

3.   *The contemporary standards
      of Lord Thomson*

There are a good many words in today's vocabulary that have
lost all meaning, and this book deals with some of them – words
like "freedom," "security," "democracy," and "welfare." *Progress*
is such a word. There was a time when the physical evidence of
construction – the raising of a barn, the draining of a swamp, the
building of a road – really *did* stand for progress. This is no longer
axiomatic.

To the Canadian business and political establishment, however, progress continues to be measured in material things and
success to be judged in terms of dollars. Mayors and aldermen
continue to boast about the height of new skyscrapers, the acreage
of new shopping plazas, the total mileage of new expressways. Is
Toronto "ahead" of Montreal? Not this year. Montreal has more
tall buildings. But wait! The Toronto-Dominion Bank is building
the highest skyscraper in the British Commonwealth! Panic over
at the Canadian Imperial Bank of Commerce which *used* to have
the highest skyscraper in the British Commonwealth! It must build
a higher one: then maybe Toronto will be ahead of Montreal.
Nobody seems to think of measuring a city's progress in terms of
its park space, or the comparative breadth of its boulevards, or the
number of trees still alive in the downtown area, or the size and
number of public squares, or the amount of its public housing, or
the recognition awarded to its artists. But then parks are for idlers,
trees block traffic, there is no tax assessment on public squares,
and the quality of a painting is not taken into account in the Gross
National Product.

The idea that a new building equals progress continues to
obsess bank presidents and aldermen. It does not seem to matter
that the presence of skyscrapers can sòmetimes hold back progress
by contributing to very real problems of traffic congestion and
human disorientation. The physical presence of the building itself
is enough. This attitude persists among municipal politicians when

public housing developments are planned and has led in the past to heartache and protest.

"The politicians can see only the buildings; they don't give a damn about the people," declares Vance Davis, a social worker who acted as relocation officer on one of two Toronto urban renewal projects. In both these projects – the Trefann Court project and the Don Mount project – the city plunged blithely ahead, expropriating homes and tearing them down with little effort to prepare the people involved for the shock of their lives. When Davis tried to organize the home owners to fight city hall and get some guarantees that they would be relocated in housing equivalent to that which was lost, he was told his services would no longer be required.

The politicians involved could not seem to get into their heads the truth that this was not simply a housing problem: it was a people problem. The homes being razed weren't worth much: but the people being ousted couldn't get equivalent housing for the price the city was paying them. They were told they'd have priority in the new housing units being built, but these units did not exist. Moreover, because more open space was certainly required in what had been a crowded slum area, there weren't going to be enough units to house all the people who had lived there. Some would have to go elsewhere – but at what cost? The general municipal attitude of mind – that you don't give poor people free dollars – mitigated against a sane and humane solution to the problem. When the people began to crowd into the council chamber shouting slogans and carrying placards, the city fathers seemed genuinely baffled and annoyed. They'd paid a fair price for the houses, hadn't they? Then what was all the fuss about?

If big buildings are the yardstick of a community's progress, then material success is the yardstick of an individual's progress. That disarmingly frank Canadian, Lord Thomson of Fleet, has said so repeatedly. He says he makes far more money than he can ever spend because it stamps him in his fellows' eyes as successful. And so it does. After all, who but Lord Thomson was selected to open the Canadian National Exhibition in 1966?

It ought to be noted that it is the *making* of money that is the yardstick of success, not the spending of it. It is often held to Lord

Thomson's credit that he acts "just like anyone else." He does not live lavishly and apart from the accumulation of newspapers and money, he seems to have few interests or pleasures. Food, wine, high living, travel for enjoyment, art, music, yachts, girls – none of these delights of flesh or spirit seems to appeal to him. If they did it is much less likely that he would have been asked to open the CNE. He would be dismissed as a "playboy" and that would be the end of that.

A similar yardstick is applied to Canadian institutions as disparate as the United Appeal and the Canadian Broadcasting Corporation. If the Appeal is to be successful, it *must* go over the top and so the top is carefully adjusted each year by the business establishment to conform to reality. In order to preserve their reputation as successes, the business leaders who run the Appeal set a goal they know can be reached. It does not seem to matter that this goal bears no relation to the real needs of the community the Appeal is supposed to serve, that the visits of neighbourhood workers may be curtailed, that the budget of the John Howard Society helping to rehabilitate ex-convicts may be cut, that needed social workers cannot be hired, and that essential services (which the business establishment insists remain in private hands) be undermined. The Appeal must be seen to be "successful."

As for the CBC, it is considered to be a failure because it continues to show a dollar-and-cents loss each year. Large numbers of people cannot be persuaded that a public broadcasting network has more important goyls than showing a profit. It is possible to hope that there will be a future generation which will look back on our time in wonder that the most important educational system yet developed should have been treated as no more than an extension of the advertising business and, in effect, denied to the schools. Television *must* show a profit; that is the prevailing view. *Ergo*, its prime function must be as a sales tool.

This tendency, to see all progress in terms of material gain and economic growth, is a distinguishing mark of the business establishment. The much-touted Gross National Product is defined entirely in material terms: in wages, salaries and incomes, investments and rents, plus the total value of goods produced. We worship the GNP yearly; it is the standard by which we judge our civilization; but it does not tell us very much about ourselves. When we talk about natural resources, we think again in material terms: pulp and paper, wheat and hydro power, oil and mineral wealth, fish and lumber. Yet people are also a natural resource; physical health, brains, talent, artistic genius – all these things are part of our true Gross National Product. It may be difficult to measure these things and add them up into some kind of yardstick but it is not impossible. The GNP of education, for instance, *can* be measured, and in dollar-and-cents terms that the business mind understands, but nobody has bothered to do it in this country. Had it been done we might have today a better and more democratic educational system. It would not be easy, but neither would it be impossible to measure the Gross National Product of our literature, music, and painting and stack it up against that of other countries. For these things, along with dollars and cents and the production of bicycles and farm machinery, are part of our real wealth.

It is significant that we measure what we call our "standard of living" in purely American terms; and when we say that we have the second highest standard of living in the world (or the third) we simply mean that *if we accept the United States' methods of measurement* then we are second or third best. But there are alternative standards of living based on scales that do not exclusively chart the consumption of goods and services. One such standard, for instance, might attempt to chart the average amount of true leisure time enjoyed by Canadians in comparison with other countries. In this chart we would, I suspect, be well down on the list. Another might conceivably deal with the amount and quality of our education. A real standard of living, surely, would take both into account. The phrase itself can be deceptive. A country with a high standard of living can number, within its population, millions of ill-fed people wearing second-hand clothes jammed into rented cubicles. Canada happens to be such a country. A standard of living index that takes into account the lowest common denominator in a society or which measures the gaps between the classes would also make an interesting study.

In the same way, phrases like "economic progress" can be illusory. As John Kenneth Galbraith has pointed out, economic growth not only fails to solve many social problems, but it also creates new ones. It doesn't provide the new and improved public services required by a higher level of public consumption; it doesn't solve the problems of urban environment (it worsens them), and it doesn't help those people who, because of their race, their lack of education, their early environment, their geographical location, their health, their age, their family situation, or their mental state, can't participate in the economy or its gains. It's not good enough to dismiss these people as drones; if the country is to be viewed in terms of what it produces then people themselves are product. If this year's crop is uneven, sickly, weak, or undeveloped then it is good business to do something about next year's crop. And that requires investment.

4. *A subtreasury of*

great Canadian myths

A study of its public pronouncements, many of which are quoted in this book, makes it clear that the business establishment pays lip service to the Puritan ethic and continues to present as realities copy-book maxims that have long since become obsolete or are about to become so.

Some of these continuing myths are religious ones. Some deal with sexual morals. Some have to do with a long outdated patriotism. "My country, right or wrong!" lost all its force after the Nuremburg and Eichmann trials. Who wants to shout slogans fouled up by the beasts of Auschwitz and Belsen? And "sex outside of marriage is sinful" has been shattered by the birth control pill.

Here are some others:

"A woman's place is in the home."

"Satan finds more mischief still for idle hands to do."

"Too much security kills initiative."

"Government planning is a denial of freedom."

"Anyone who works hard will rise to the top."

"It's your own fault if you're poor."

"Hard work is the backbone of the nation."

"Free enterprise means unlimited opportunity for all."

"Anyone can work his way through college."

"Higher taxes will wreck the nation."

"Private property must be sacrosanct."

All of these statements can be heard any day of the week. They continue to be the basis of newspaper editorials. They find their way into annual reports and presidential addresses. The official pronouncements of the business establishment have made them gospel. Many a luncheon-club speaker assumes his listeners take them for granted.

But all are open to challenge, and it is the purpose of this book to challenge them. Actually, many of the old saws reproduced above represent a kind of doublethink on the part of those who use them. Industrial leaders and their spokesmen parrot them as priests parrot the Apostles' Creed; threaded together they form a comfortable liturgy, a wistful link to those dear, dead days when there was truth in them. Businessmen repeat them over and over again to each other, scarcely understanding their meaning, like missionaries preaching to the converted. Often enough they demonstrate by their actions that they no longer believe what they are saying.

A good example is the so-called sacrosanct nature of private property. Our attitudes to private property are changing more swiftly than we know. In the summer of 1967, at the thinkers' conference for the Progressive Conservative Party, a leading builder indicated in public what many of his colleagues had been saying in private for some time: that private property, in the narrow sense of land ownership, is virtually obsolete. Politicians being what they are, it is scarcely likely that any party, including the New Democrats, will embody the expropriation of urban real estate into its platform. Nonetheless in the light of today's appalling land speculation, there is an excellent case for it.

The water is publicly owned; no one but the people have title to Lake Ontario or the St. Lawrence River. The air is publicly owned; can anyone imagine entrepreneurs speculating in acreages of air space? And today most hydro power is owned publicly. Then why not the land?

The harping on private ownership is one of the root causes of our really pressing urban problems. It inhibits, indeed it defeats, any attempt at intelligent city planning. The problem of land assembly, even for a few city blocks, is so complicated it is frightening. Our cities continue to grow haphazardly because everyone wants the right to do with his land what he pleases; and, in spite of some primitive zoning by-laws, he generally does pretty much as he pleases. Since we must all live or work in the city, we are all losers here. Whether we own a city lot or a city block or merely work in an office building, we are surrounded by unsightliness and ugliness; we are cramped by an anarchy that inhibits movement and promotes discomfort. Many of us spend well over half our waking hours in the blighted downtown areas – more time than we spend in our own homes; and yet, because of this attitude toward private property, we cannot control our own surroundings and make them pleasing to us. Is this freedom? What is the use of wealth, position, or power if we live and work among discomfort and ugliness? These things are meaningless as long as we value real estate more than we do environment.

The continuing emphasis on private property is costing most of us hard cash. We are pouring it by the shovelful into the coffers of the land speculators. This artificial increase in the land values of the major cities is making everything more expensive. Not only is it shooting up the prices of homes to the point where millions cannot afford to build; not only is it sky-rocketing apartment rents to the point where people must flee to a strangely unsatisfying half-world on the outskirts of the city; but it is also having its effect on other goods. If the supermarkets pay more for land, then food prices must rise. Thus the cost of city living goes up and up and the only ones who profit are a minority of speculators who contribute nothing at all to the community in the way of production. Such people are the real drones of society.

In the course of preparing this book, I twice lunched with

groups of people interested in housing and planning: architects, town planners, builders. All were unanimous on this matter of the public ownership of land and no wonder; the facts support them.

In 1955, for instance, land on St. George Street, a relatively good location in downtown Toronto, was selling for the equivalent of $1,000 per apartment unit. By 1967, similarly located land had risen to between $3,000 and $4,000 per apartment unit.

In 1955, a semi-detached lot in a reasonably close-in location in the Toronto suburb of Scarborough would cost a builder around $2,200 per dwelling unit. *By 1967 this cost had risen to $8,000.*

In both these instances, we are faced with a rise in land costs of around 350 per cent.

It is interesting to compare this phenomenal rise in the cost of land with the rise in other construction costs, labour, and materials. A comparison is available for the period between 1959 and 1967 during which labour, construction, and material costs rose between fifteen per cent (for houses) and twenty per cent (for apartment buildings). In the same period the price of a 120-acre parcel of land in a relatively good location in Metropolitan Toronto rose from $6,000 an acre to $27,000 an acre. This is an increase of 270 per cent. It is a high price to pay to support an old principle.

An alternative would be for the government to own all real estate, retain what it needed for roads, parks, and its own use in planning the cities, and then lease the rest back for varying periods to the people at controlled prices. It is all right to suggest such things at thinkers' conferences, but one can imagine the hue and cry that would go up if a practical politician proposed it. *"Socialize the land? Ye Gods, you strike at the very root of our freedom!"* (How often the word "freedom" is dragged out to perpetuate the *status quo*!) On occasion I have made a similar suggestion in the course of a speech and every time I mention the idea I can hear a ripple of horror running through the audience. It is almost as bad as suggesting that a really free people ought to have the option of lying in the sun and drinking beer, or that the day is coming when savings and life insurance may both be obsolete.

5. *The contempt for*
   adult values

"This generation," says Marshall McLuhan, "lives mystically and in depth." In this sense it differs radically from past generations. There has always been a gap of sorts between the old and the young but never a gap of such proportions as exists today. It is obvious that large numbers of the new generation of the Sixties no longer subscribe to the old ethic, and that they feel a sense of frustration with those members of the older generation who continue to do so.

Some of these are existentialists who are not concerned with the future in the Puritan sense. Some are hippies who reject the work ethic of the Calvinists and the profit-based materialism of Western society. Some are activists and idealists who believe that the individual is not sufficient unto himself, that every man is his brother's keeper, and that in a really democratic society the Puritan family unit has to be extended to cover the full community. In one way or another they reject the rigid values of the establishment – an establishment, be it said, that includes liberals as well as conservatives and socialists as well as capitalists.

My own view is that much of this contempt for adult values springs directly from television, the propaganda arm of the business establishment. Television has rendered the young infinitely more sophisticated, but those who control the medium are apparently not aware of that fact. The commercial messages, in large part, are clearly aimed at the unsophisticated. For twenty years television commercials have taught the young to be suspicious – nay, cynical – of adult pronouncements. Any message that can seriously purport to show that a random sample of adult citizens cannot tell the difference between a drink made from packaged crystals and real orange juice is bound to inculcate in the alert young viewer a considerable scepticism.

In the same way the new generation today listens with cynicism to the old generation prattle publicly about "freedom," perhaps the most overworked word in the post-war lexicon of luncheon club clichés. The continual boasting about our free institutions is not lost upon a generation which wants, but is often denied, a large measure of its own kind of freedom.

A few days before Christmas, 1966, a twenty-three-year-old guitarist named Franklin Hamilton appeared before a Vancouver magistrate and was ordered to get his hair cut. The alternative, said the magistrate, was a day in jail. There is no law of the land that sets any length on hair and there would be a national outcry if such a law were proposed; and yet the law in this case forced a man to alter his personal appearance simply to appease a jurist's whim. "I have a particular propensity against long hair," said the magistrate, whose name is Gerald Levey.

In vain Hamilton protested that the length of his hair affected his ability to make money since he was a musician and it was, in effect, part of his costume. This did not move the magistrate.

"I'm a musician too," said Mr. Levey. "I have a degree. You can buy a wig."

This is not an isolated case. All over the country there are cases of young men being ordered by the courts to get their hair cut. Canadian Press reported from Montreal that same fall: "Judge J. Redmond Roche made it clear that young men with shoulder-length hair have two strikes against them when they appear in court before him." The judge, who already knew the answer, had just asked a youth if he were a man or a girl, and when the defendant replied that he was a man the judge snapped that he didn't agree with him and gave him a summary ten days in jail on a shoplifting charge.

This attitude was given quasi-official sanction in the July, 1967, issue of *The Ontario Magistrate's Quarterly*, which editorialized on the subject:

"The longhairs are not just beatniks; they're dead-beats, and if growing their hair long is going to be the prevailing fashion (which, of course, it won't), we will be seeing more and more of them all the time in magistrate's courts. There is just no future for them outside the beneficent confines of the excellent penitentiaries and reformatories that are ready and willing to receive them. They will get a haircut there, all right, and very fast."

No one should be too surprised at this attitude of the courts since the whole process of law in Canada supports the propertied establishment and the propertied establishment feels itself threatened by a generation that refuses to conform to an ethic that demands an ordered and well-scrubbed uniformity, a disciplined attitude to life, a steady job, and a rigid code of conduct. Miniskirts (as a lady reporter found out in Toronto in 1967) are as much anathema to jurists as overalls, which is why good defence lawyers insist that accused rapists and murderers disguise themselves as members of the upper classes in pinstripe suits and sober ties no matter what their station.

It has long been clear whose side the law is on. Only the poor drunks go to jail. Only the Chinese social clubs are continually harassed by the gambling squad. Only the parties in the poorer districts are raided by the police. The legal system supports the evictor (be he priest or slumlord) against the evicted and the creditor against the debtor. If an illiterate housewife is hoodwinked by a glib salesman into signing a non-cancellable contract and promissory note for shoddy goods outrageously priced, the law in almost every case will be on the salesman's side. "The commercial world would soon fall apart if promissory notes were tossed out," a Toronto judge told one immigrant couple who found they owed close to $400 for a $28 Japanese-made knitting machine, sold them on the basis of a series of phoney promises. The law forced them to pay but it did not take action against the fly-by-nights who had wrung thousands of dollars from the gullible.

Is it really necessary to document the law's support of the propertied when the newspapers do the job daily? A big contractor who steals $40,000 from the public purse through income tax evasion escapes with a fine while a youth with long hair goes to jail for ten days for stealing a $35 dress. For ten years, eighteen companies monopolized the linen business in Montreal and made a mockery of the so-called free enterprise system by fixing prices to the point where anyone who bought a tablecloth was being cheated. The stiffest individual fine handed down, in March of 1967, was $5,000. But in the same year a jobless man of forty-eight was jailed for five days because he stole a ten cent newspaper.

Compare the magistrate's courts, which are the courts of the poor, with the supreme courts, where the big private property cases are heard. The courts of the poor are shoddy and crowded, the acoustics wretched, the clerks and sheriffs' officers ill-tempered, the magistrates harried and impatient ("Get on with it!" is a frequently heard instruction). By contrast, the courts of the propertied are cool and temperate palaces.

Can one really be surprised that the judges favour the established order when they themselves are chosen, often for political reasons, from the establishment? The point was made years ago by Lord Justice Scrutton in England when he admitted that impartiality was a difficult thing to attain. "I am not speaking of conscious impartiality," he said, "but the habits you are trained in, the people with whom you mix, lead you to a certain class of ideas of such nature that, when you have to deal with other ideas, you do not give as sound and accurate judgements as you would wish."

The magistrate who confessed so frankly to his particular propensity against long hair surely meant a great deal more than that, though perhaps he did not realize it. After all, another musician, Ludwig van Beethoven, had long hair. Einstein had long hair and so did Jesus Christ and most of the kings of England. There was indeed a time when magistrates had a particular propensity against *short* hair. (Oscar Wilde was considered a nonconformist because he was clean-shaven.) Long hair is only a symbol of a new attitude which makes the establishment uneasy because it is in direct conflict with the establishment ethic.

The same can be said, I think, for those controversial drugs, marijuana and LSD. Dr. Abraham Hoffer, who knows as much about LSD as anyone (he was Director of Psychiatric Research, University Hospital, Saskatoon), believes that the national hysteria against the drug is not directed against the danger to the person using it but against the danger to society as a whole. Anything that makes people turn on and drop out of the work-oriented, timetabled social organization represents a threat to the established order. "It is not the chemical," he says, "but the experience which is feared."

It is still monstrous that in a society which claims to value freedom any citizen should be told how to dress or wear his hair.

Some freedoms must be curtailed in the interests of society as a whole; considerable interference with the way people act is necessary in a complex community; but matters of fashion are nobody's business but the individual's.

Why is the educational establishment so uneasy about long hair? The key, perhaps, is to be found in the words of J. Wilkie Davey of Bathurst Heights Secondary School in Toronto who insisted that one boy get his hair cut because "education must develop followership as well as leadership . . . the very qualities insisted upon by business and industry." Or, again, in the words of the principal of a school in the Toronto suburb of Etobicoke who banned long hair because, he said, "we like them [the students] to be dressed as if they were going to business." Many a high-school principal seems to be more fanatic about "dress and deportment" than he is about the calibre of his teachers. Any departure from the conventional is discouraged. At St. Andrews Junior High School in North York, Ontario, one fifteen-year-old boy was held by two teachers while his hair was trimmed. At St. James College in Winnipeg, the order is that all must look alike: eyebrows must be exposed, ears uncovered, and the hairline must be above the collar. Sir Winston Churchill Secondary School in Vancouver is only one of many where miniskirts are banned and yet, ironically, when the miniskirt is viewed by the establishment as a school uniform it becomes perfectly acceptable. In many of the private schools in this country (where it is called a "tunic"), the miniskirt is insisted upon. Only when it becomes a symbol of youthful non-conformity is it prohibited as something sinful and distracting.

It's interesting here to consider the correlation between the idea of conformity and the idea of cleanliness. Non-conforming youths, whether hippies or peace marchers, are continually referred to by the press without any really hard evidence as "the unwashed." It is instantly assumed that long hair and beards are always filthy. Marcel Fox, the Principal of Baron Byng highschool in Montreal, talks about "messy hair reflecting messy attitudes." Yet in the same highschool almost every teenage girl wears her hair shoulder-length and nobody considers her to be unclean. College professors who sport beards and Viennese psychoanalysts who wear goatees are never considered to be anything but well-scrubbed. Highschool principals ought to know that the Puritans who landed at Plymouth Rock, in the days when cleanliness was really next to godliness, had haircuts remarkably similar to those of the Beatles. But then they were non-conformists, too.

It is ironic that the highschools, which are supposed to be inculcating the principles of freedom and democracy among the young, should themselves be totalitarian. Anyone who has been to highschool or talked recently to highschool students or who has children of his own at highschool knows that student government is a farce and that the student newspaper is so heavily censored by staff advisors that it can only be a pale reflection of adult attitudes. Indeed, in 1966, the Chairman of the Toronto Board of Education, Barry Lowes, remarked flatly that "highschool government, as we know it, is a charade." Student editors and student politicians are not allowed to learn from their own errors and follies. Students who continually ask searching questions in class are frowned on as nuisances: they take up precious time in an already crowded curriculum. Ban-the-bomb groups have had trouble forming in many highschools, and specific political discussion is often denied official sanction and must operate clandestinely. Always there is the repeated emphasis on discipline, control and order, on "good behaviour" (*i.e.*, docility) rather than on good character, on an assembly-line education, efficient but dull, designed to fit students for assembly-line jobs but scarcely calculated to turn them into thinking, questioning citizens. It seems astonishing that educators could believe that, having been drilled for all his formative years to yield without question to authority from above, a young man should be suddenly expected to make intelligent voting decisions the instant he reaches the age of twenty-one.

Here is the principal of a Leamington, Ontario, highschool being interviewed on television and defending his "quick, clear-cut, efficient policy" which he admits can never be democratic:

"We turn out a product to pass examinations, to get jobs in industry, commercial and technical. You cannot beat success, and I am rather inclined to think that this has been a successful school."

Here is a teacher writing to the Toronto *Star*:

"Pupils who succeed best in school are those who best follow a teacher's instructions and conform to their school's requirements concerning proper dress and behaviour. . . . Even teachers in order to be successful must conform to some inspector's stereotyped criteria. . . . As a teacher I feel our rebellious youth should bear in mind that conformity is usually the price of success and that reputations are injured rather than enhanced by flouting social convention."

Here is an open letter from the staff of the student newspaper at Alderwood Collegiate near Toronto explaining why they have resigned:

At the Alder Echo *meeting we said that we could get an interview with a civil rights worker from Alabama and we were told that articles on controversial issues were not allowed. Since then the administration has gone on and told the* Alder Echo *to limit itself to articles not political or religious, not controversial or topical, not serious or significant, not dangerous to the common happy lives that students are taught to lead. The* Alder Echo *must be a trivial sheet of dead issues. We can talk about coloured stockings but not about coloured people.*

Is all this too extreme a view of the educational system? Are these merely isolated cases? I think not. In my own profession I meet a good many highschool editors, and what saddens me most is their resigned attitude to adult censorship. Few of them have the temerity of the staff of the *Alder Echo*. "Oh, they won't let us say that," they often remark, as if the matter were a closed issue. The idea of saying it anyway and damn the consequences, of arguing the point with the teachers, of starting a clandestine newspaper – these things do not seem to occur to any of them. It may be true, as Barry Lowes has said, that many of these seemingly docile students resent the system bitterly and are quietly figuring out a way to grab power; but it seems more likely that large numbers of the brightest non-conformists are simply dropping out from boredom and frustration.

The idea that education should be participatory, even at the university level, is anathema to the educational establishment which wants neither truck nor trade with the idea that students should have some representation on the governing bodies of universities. The students at the University of Western Ontario almost managed to achieve this, after a long and bitter struggle, but the idea was shot down in flames by the Ontario legislature. Yet why shouldn't a student or two be on the governing body which is often enough packed with businessmen who have never seen the inside of a lecture hall and whose only criterion for inclusion is that they have made a lot of money? In this area as in so many others, the establishment is fighting a rearguard action; the old adage that children should be seen and not heard belongs to a dying ethic.

On the campus the establishment seems to be concerned with pretty much same trivia that concerns the highschool principals. For this we have the evidence of Professor John Seeley, a distinguished Canadian sociologist, formerly a faculty member at both the University of Toronto and York University and now Director of the Centre of Democratic Study at Santa Barbara. Here is his description of what the academic establishment worries about:

Whether students should wear ties to classes and jackets to dinner; how high should be the dias on which rests the high table; whether Business Administration needs a separate school or should be administratively subordinate to this or that; whether to allow smoking at Senate meetings or to charge professors as well as students for parking; how many credits to allow home economics; just where which dean should march in a procession.

And what does the university administrator worry about? Again, Professor Seeley:

How to secure image; how to ensure money to permit size and growth in order to multiply power . . . whether the university president shall have a house and a university car . . . how to control the campus newspaper without the appearance of so doing; and how to subvert such student government as there is so that it "freely" becomes an accomplice to the institutional plans and schemes.

The old-line educators are as confused and as angered by the student demands for more freedom as the judges are by long hair and the police by marijuana. They long for the days when young people minded their elders ("betters" was the word, wasn't it?), did exactly what they were told, dressed neatly in cap and gown, and scribbled away in their books when the teacher dictated notes from behind the desk of authority. These days, astonishingly, have not yet gone, but their death knell has been sounded and this is why there is tension on the campus. Last-ditch defences are always the most vehement. People become violently patriotic and imperialistic just before an empire disintegrates; royalists become rampant just before the throne collapses; religious argument flares up as the prelude to a dying creed.

In Toronto in 1967 there was modestly opened a free university, Rochdale College, which is concerned with the humanities and which rejects the tyranny of examinations, time tables, and entrance requirements. It does not grant degrees and it provides no prescribed lectures in the traditional sense. Its central principle is that decisions are taken by the people whom they affect and that these people must live with the results of their own decisions, modifying them where they see fit. Students and faculty together decide upon fees and curriculum. Each member of the college is responsible for the direction, method, and pace of his studies. As the brochure points out, "The college has no way of knowing whether prospective employers will be impressed by a member's achievement at Rochdale."

Obviously, this is not a university for just anybody; its undergraduates must be more concerned with knowledge than with getting a job, and they themselves must observe some highly personal discipline which requires a higher kind of individual responsibility than that demanded by the assembly-line campus. If it is the university of the future it also bears, significantly, a suspicious resemblance to the mediaeval universities of the past which existed in the days before the Puritan ethic made knowledge a means to an end and a job an end in itself.

6. *Charles E. Wilson's version of freedom*

The phrase "free university" is significant because, traditionally, all universities are supposed to be bastions of freedom. The word "freedom" has had such a working-over during two post-war decades that it has become almost meaningless. "Our basic freedoms" . . . "our free way of life" . . . "the freedoms we enjoy" . . . who has not heard these phrases rolling glibly from the tongues of politicians and public speakers? And who has not heard that all-encompassing phrase "the free world," a world which includes such nations as Portugal where freedom is spat upon and trampled? With all this talk of freedom, who can blame the new generation for demanding more? For this is exactly what they are asking for: freedom to dress the way they wish, freedom to use their own brands of intoxicant, freedom to demonstrate in the streets, freedom to speak and read and see without censorship, to spout poetry in the parks, to sleep around if they wish to, to walk the streets shoeless without police interference, and to question the major values of adult society.

But this is not the kind of freedom the smug minority talks about when its members gather together for tribal incantations.

Charles E. Wilson, President of General Motors, addresses the Empire Club in Toronto in January 1951 and tells it what it wants to hear:

"For more than one hundred and fifty years, free men in our countries have had the opportunities to educate themselves, choose their own religions, select their own occupations, accumulate capital, and invent better ways of doing things. The reason the people of our countries are relatively more prosperous results from the simple fact that, by accepting the challenge of individual competition as a responsibility that comes with personal freedom, we have done a better job of applying our human energy and individual initiative to the improvement, not only of ourselves, but of all. . . . Our political systems that permit and promote individual enterprise, personal responsibility, free competition, respect for the rights of others, freedom of choice and decision, freedom itself, are the final important factors that make the difference between our country and others."

H. Gordon Love, President of the Canadian Chamber of Commerce, speaks to the forty-eighth annual meeting of the U.S. Chamber, attacks the welfare state, and praises "those tried and proved weapons – the resourcefulness of individual freedom and individual enterprise":

"We must cherish freedom, understand it, believe in it, and desire it so strongly that nothing will shake our purpose to maintain it and expand it."

The Chamber of Commerce bulletin fires an editorial salvo for freedom in February, 1964:

"Thanks to a political and economic system which makes us the free-est people in the world, we find ourselves with a per capita wealth second only to the people of the U.S. . . . We have been successful because we have recognized the virtues and values of the economic system of competitive private enterprise. Men have been freed to exercise their skills, their ingenuity, their enterprise in the fields which interest them most."

It is quite clear that the freedoms meant here are of a very special kind and have very little to do with the nature of the freedoms upon which the new generation is insisting. When businessmen talk about freedom they do not mean free love, they mean the freedom under *laissez-faire* enterprise to operate with the minimum of government interference, to charge the highest prices the market will bear, to pay the lowest wages they can get away with, and to organize cosy little monopolies without federal snooping. These freedoms include freedom from higher taxation, freedom to choose one's own charities (or none at all), and freedom from government regulation. It is a nice kind of freedom if you're Charlie Wilson, but for large numbers of people it has no meaning at all.

Unfair! scream the businessmen. *Untrue! There is government regulation and we don't object to it. There are laws against monopolies and we go along with them. Unions regulate hours and wages and the government sets minimum wages and we accept all that. We simply think things have gone far enough. We don't want further interference. We don't want the welfare state to go any further. If it does, then we say that freedom is in jeopardy.*

Well, all right. And it is also true that all the things the business establishment now says it accepts, from the right to organize to the eight-hour day, it once opposed vehemently as an erosion of freedom or an economic impossibility. It has been dragged kicking and screaming down the road to social progress, crying out at every step that we have gone far enough, that it is time to call a halt, that anything new will wreck the country. And always it has yammered about freedom.

Most of the time when people mouth clichés about our "free society," they mean that we are politically free. And so we are to a considerable extent, more so than most peoples in the world. Yet even in this sense we are not as free as we think or as free as we could be. Westerners are always boasting to Communists about their right to boo their country's leaders. But in the summer of 1967, a young art critic named Barry Lord discovered he wasn't free to utter aloud a dissenting political opinion on Canadian soil. When Lord shouted the words "murderer" and "bloody butcher" at Lyndon Johnson during the United States President's visit to Expo '67, he was immediately seized by four plainclothesmen, manhandled, punched, held for seven hours, and ultimately fined one hundred dollars for disturbing the peace. As Lord remarked later, quoting Bertrand Russell, "I had my freedom until I needed it." (Interestingly enough, similar phrases have been shouted periodically at various East European political leaders and representatives visiting Canada without police interference.) And, in 1967, an anti-establishment newspaper was banned in Vancouver, without a trial, by the simple expedient of cancelling its business licence.

The right to free speech and free expression in Canada is hedged around with a variety of subtly inhibiting factors, many of them economic. A very large proportion of Canadians are afraid of being outspoken because of the fear – a real one – of losing their jobs if they express unorthodox opinions. When I was a newspaper columnist, I received letters every day expressing views on a variety of subjects from people who asked me not to use their names for that reason.

It is true that in a Communist country any man who publicly expresses consistent capitalist leanings will find himself in trouble and probably in jail. It is equally true that anyone who publicly expresses consistent Communist opinions in Canada will find himself out of a job, socially ostracized, and economically strangled.

Still, we can vote, we can write letters to the press, we can talk and argue freely, we can (if we can afford it) publish and distribute pamphlets, buy radio and newspaper space for unpopular causes, carry signs of protest (as long as we have a permit and don't commit the awful crime of interfering with traffic), and, in one or two places, even stand up on soap boxes and make speeches (as long as we don't cause a riot). And we cannot be jailed for our views.

But there are other freedoms denied to large numbers of Canadians, and to many these freedoms are just as important, perhaps more important, than the periodical freedom to vote or to dissent. When Charles Wilson tells Canadians that free men here have the opportunity to educate themselves, to select their own occupations, and to accumulate capital, he is perpetuating one of the great myths of the age. The truth is that large numbers of men and women have not had the opportunity to educate themselves to the limits of their mental abilities. The truth is that twenty-five per cent of all adult Canadians have not been able to accumulate any liquid capital at all. The truth is that an army of people are working in jobs which are not really of their own choosing and which can only be described as degrading. None of these people can be said to be free in the proper sense of that overworked and mangled word.

A poor man is not free and a destitute man is as much a prisoner as a convict; indeed a convict generally eats better. A man who can't afford a streetcar ticket, let alone real travel, who can exercise no real choice in matters of food, clothing, and shelter, who cannot follow the siren song of the TV commercials, who can scarcely afford bus fare to the library let alone a proper education for himself or his children – is such a man free in an affluent nation? There are such men and women in Canada and their numbers are legion. Until there is a basic economic floor beneath them, these people cannot begin to participate in the whole range of what we mean when we talk glibly about a free society.

The business establishment believes, or pretends to believe, that the provision of such a floor would somehow be an invasion of liberty. Too much security, it is argued, weakens the fibre of the nation. A better case can be made for the fact that the only free men are the secure men. Dr. Morton Shulman, the notorious Toronto coroner, on whom a successful television series has been based, was able to speak up freely on a variety of important subjects largely because he didn't give a damn about losing his job. He had made all the money he needed in the stock and bond market and so was secure enough to hit out at the establishment and, when the establishment fired him, to run for political office. Often we hear municipal politicians talking about the necessity of raising the salaries of aldermen so that "good men can run for office." The matter came up at the same conference of mayors and reeves that bitterly attacked welfare payments for the poor. What the mayors were really saying was: "We must have more free men in power."

My friend, John Farina, who is Deputy Director of the University of Toronto's School of Social Work, suggested in his master's thesis that leisure was a synonym for freedom. Leisure, in Aristotle's phrase, is "the state of being free from the *necessity* of labour" (the italics are mine). But Farina also pointed out that true leisure, as opposed to "free time," presupposed two things: the freedom to choose what one does and the *capacity* to choose what one does. Without these two prerequisites, true leisure and true freedom are not possible.

A man who spends half his waking hours performing tasks which he hates and the remainder of the time fulfilling duties which irk or bore him can scarcely be called free. He is, in this society, the slave to an outmoded ethic. But the capacity to choose, as Farina pointed out, is related to knowledge. An uneducated man – a man who has not been able to fulfil his own potential – cannot be said to be free; he is fettered as surely as a convict. And any society that does not provide equal opportunity for all men and women to educate themselves to the utmost of their ability cannot be called a totally free society.

That is really what this book is all about: freedom, and the lack of it, in all its multitudinous guises . . . freedom from want and sudden disaster . . . freedom from foolish toil . . . freedom from ignorance. In the New Democracy, these freedoms ought to be as basic as the right to vote or to boo the Prime Minister or to call a foreign statesman a bloody butcher, even on the hallowed soil of a world exposition.

TWO **_The mythology_**
of toil

Who first invented work, and bound the free

And holyday-rejoicing spirit down

To the ever-haunting importunity

Of business in the green fields, and the town –

To plough, loom, anvil, spade – and oh! most sad

To that dry drudgery at the desk's dead wood?

Charles Lamb

1.   *The dirtiest job*

       in the world

On my seventeenth birthday, which fell on July 12, 1937, one of the
worst years of the Depression, I went to work for pay and there
was jubilation among my friends and relatives. In an era when jobs
were scarce I had a job; and having a job was the goal of everyone
in those days. Having a job in the Thirties was a bit like having a
swimming pool in the Sixties; it conferred status. It didn't really
matter what the job was. It could be unrewarding, mindless, foolish, unproductive, even degrading – no matter: it set you apart as
a paying member of a society whose creed was that everyone must
work at something, and the harder the better, too.

My job was in a mining camp in the Yukon some 1,500 miles
from my home in Victoria, B.C. I worked ten hours a day, seven
days a week, and I was paid $4.50 a day plus my board. Almost
everybody who learned about my job had the same thing to say
about it: "It will make a man out of you!" And when the job came
to an end at the start of my university term, almost every adult I
knew examined my hands to note with satisfaction the heavy cal-
louses. Back-breaking work was considered to be a high form of
human endeavour. A man who worked hard couldn't be all bad,
whether he was a convict breaking rocks in a prison yard or an
executive neglecting his family by toiling weekends at the office.

I worked for three summer seasons at that same job and it was
commonly held that I was "working my way through college,"
another laudable endeavour in a society which believed, and still
believes, that every individual must pay his own way regardless of
position, health, mental ability, or physical condition.

The first year I worked on a construction gang; the following
years I worked on the thawing crew, engaged in preparing the
ground for the actual gold mining that was to follow. Thawing
permafrost with cold water is a fascinating process to almost
everyone except those actually employed in it. As far as I know, it

is the world's muddiest job, involving as it does the pumping of millions of gallons of cold water into the bowels of the earth.

In earlier days steam had been used to thaw the permanently frozen ground so that the dredges could reach the gold; but the lovely, verdant valleys had long since been denuded of their timber and no fuel was left to operate the old-time boilers. So now a new process had been devised to tear the valley apart and convert it into a heaving sea of mud.

On Dominion Creek in the Klondike watershed, where I toiled those three Depression summers, the gold lay hidden in crevices of bedrock some twenty or thirty feet beneath the surface. The valley was perhaps a mile wide at this point and it was being ripped to pieces so that man might reach this gold. First, every shred of plant life was sheared off by a bush-cutting crew. Then all the black topsoil, most of it frozen hard as granite, was sluiced away by giant nozzles flinging water against the banks at a pressure so high it could cut a man in half. By the time the thawing crew arrived, the sinuous valley, misty green each spring, flaming orange each fall, had been reduced to a black, glistening scar.

It was our task to dam the creek anew to build up water pressure and then introduce a spider web of pipes across the newly ravaged valley floor. From these pipes at sixteen-foot intervals there protruded an octopus-like tangle of hoses. On to each hose was fastened a ten-foot length of pipe, known as a "point," because of the chisel-bit at the end. This point was driven into the frozen soil by means of a slide hammer. When it was down the full ten feet, an extension pipe was screwed onto the end and this was driven down, too, inch by painful inch. If necessary, further extensions were added. And all the time, without cessation, ice cold water was being pumped through every pipe at high pressure. In this way an underground lake was created beneath the valley floor and, though its waters were only a few degrees above freezing, that small change in temperature was enough to thaw the permafrost.

And so we toiled away, up to our ankles, our knees, and sometimes even our hips in a pulsating gruel of mud and ice-water. The men who drove those points into the rock-like soil were soaking wet most of the time, for it was difficult to add extensions or withdraw a point without water spurting in all directions. All day long they laboured, with their fingers curled around the handles of their slide hammers, their torsos rising and falling as they drove each pipe inch by inch into the earth. When a point became plugged it had to be hauled up and unplugged while the ice-water squirted in their faces. Each man was logged on the amount of footage he had driven in a day, and if that footage was seen to be too low he could expect to draw his time slip that evening. There was a story current in my day that the general manager had come out from Dawson on a tour of inspection and seen a man standing immobile in the distance. "Fire that man!" he cried. "I've been watching him and he hasn't moved for half an hour." Later it was discovered that he *couldn't* move; he was up to his hips in mud.

As the water continued to flow into the ground, the floor of the valley began to go to pieces. Immense craters ten or twenty feet deep began to appear. Whole sections fell away, sometimes taking men with them. The mud grew thicker. The pipeline supports toppled as the soil crumbled, and the pipes themselves – mainlines and feeder lines – began to buckle and break and to shoot icy fountains in every direction. When this occurred it was the job of the pipeline crew, of which I was a member, to replace the pilings, drive new pipes and repair leaks. Sometimes the sun was out and we stripped to our shorts; sometimes a bone-chilling wind swept down the valley accompanied by a sleety rain. It did not matter. We worked our ten hours (later it was reduced to a merciful nine) day in and day out, without a holiday of any kind.

When you work for ten hours at hard labour, whether you are seventeen or fifty-seven, there is precious little time or energy left for anything else. We rose at six, performed our swift ablutions, wolfed an enormous breakfast, and headed off for the job which had to begin at seven. At noon we started back up the valley slopes through the mud to the messhall, wolfed another vast meal, and finished it just in time to head back once more. At six we were finished, in more ways than one. I have seen men so tired they could not eat the final meal of the day which was always con- sumed in silence and at top speed. (It was said that any man who stumbled on the messhall steps on the way in found himself trampled by the rush coming out.) When this was over, large numbers of men of varying ages simply lay down on their bunks, utterly fagged out, and slept. There was nothing else to do any- way: no library, no recreation hall, no lounge, no radio or films – nothing but a roadhouse five miles distant where you could buy bootleg rum. Civilization was represented by Dawson, forty miles away; we never visited it. We were like men in a prison camp, except that we worked much harder.

Under such conditions any kind of creative act or thought is difficult. I remember one man, a German immigrant, who was trying to learn to draw by correspondence. He had some talent but in the end he had to give it up. He was too tired to draw. I had brought along a pile of books required in my university course for summer reading, but most of the time I found I was too tired to read. Those who did not immediately go to sleep after supper spent their spare time washing their work clothes or lying in their bunks indulging in verbal sexual fantasies. I often wondered if this was what the adults meant when they said that mining camp life would make a man of me. Certainly I learned a great deal more from these sexual bull sessions than I had at my mother's knee. It was not until many years later that I discovered most of it was wrong.

It is difficult to describe the absolute dreariness and hopeless- ness of this kind of job. The worst thing about it was that there was no respite, since – in a seven-day-a-week job – there were no breaks of any kind to look forward to until the coming of winter rendered further toil impossible. There was one wit among us who used to leap from his bunk once a week, when the bull cook banged the triangle at 6:00 A.M., crying jubilantly: "Thank God, it's Sunday!" This always provoked a bitter laugh. Without any change of pace, time moves sluggishly; without any break in the routine, a kind of lethargy steals over the mind. The blessed winter seemed eons away to all of us.

Yet for me, in my late teens, life in this mining camp was immeasurably easier than it was for the others. There were men here in their sixties who had lived this way all their lives. There were men in their prime with wives and children to support – families they did not see for half of every year. There were all kinds of men here and few who were really stupid. I worked with immigrants from Austria, Germany, Switzerland, Italy, Sweden,

Norway, and Denmark, as well as with Canadians. Most were intelligent and a great many were extremely sharp and able. All were industrious. Each had displayed enough courage and independence to somehow make his way several thousand miles to the one corner of North America where a job of sorts was comparatively easy to get. But all had one thing in common: according to my observation, none had been educated up to his ability.

There were many men in that mining camp easily capable of obtaining a university degree; and there were many more who might have completed highschool and then gone on to technical school. I saw them each evening, lying on their bunks and trying to force their hands open – hands that had been curled into almost permanent positions around cold pipes; I saw them each morning, shambling down to that grotesque mudpie of a valley; during the day I saw them – scores of ant-like figures, bent double over their slide hammers, struggling in the gumbo, striving and groaning; and the thought that came to my mind was ever the same: "What a waste of human resources!"

For this "job," which everybody had congratulated me upon getting, which was supposed to be so ennobling, which was to make a man of me, was actually degrading, destructive, and above all useless. It was degrading because it reduced men to the status of beasts. There was one wag who went around with his zipper purposely undone and his genitals exposed. "If I'm working like a horse, I might as well look like one," he'd say. It was destructive because it reduced a glorious setting to a black obscenity. And it was useless because the gold, which was mined at such expense and human cost, was melted into bars and shipped to Fort Knox in the United States where it was once again confined below ground. Every manjack of us knew this; it was the subject of much bitter banter and wisecracking; each of us, I think, was disturbed by the fact that we were engaged in an operation which was essentially unproductive. If we'd been growing wheat, we would at least have had the satisfaction of knowing our labours were useful. The whole, vast, complicated operation seemed to me to be pointless: even the stockholders failed to profit by it greatly; for years the company was forced to pass its dividends. Would we or the nation have been worse off if we had stayed drunk all summer?

For myself, as a teenager, there were certain minor advantages that did not apply to those older men who worked out of necessity and desperation. Certainly it was healthy enough. Certainly I got to know a bit more about my fellow men. It occurs to me now, however, that both these goals could have been achieved in a pleasanter and more productive fashion. As for the financial gain, much of that was illusory. After I paid for my equipment and my return fare home, there was precious little left. The first year I scarcely broke even. In succeeding seasons I was able to pay my university tuition but not much more. Like my fellow students, I could say that I was working my way through college, but like most of them I could not have continued a university career had I not been able to board at home and take money for clothing and extras from my parents. During four years at university, I met only a handful of students who were able to support themselves wholly through summer employment.

The one valuable asset that I recovered from my mining camp experience was status. It allows me to use a line in my official biography which I notice is seized upon joyfully by those who have to introduce me when I make after-dinner speeches: "During the Thirties, he worked in Yukon mining camps to help put himself through university." When that line is uttered the audience is prepared to forgive me almost anything: outlandishly radical opinions, dangerous views on matters sexual, alarming attitudes toward religion. I am pronounced worthy because, in that one sentence, is summed up the great Canadian myth: that work – *any* work – is the most important thing in life, and that anybody who is willing to work hard enough can by his own initiative get as far as he wants.

2.   *The second coming*

      of Aristotle

In spite of scientific prognostications that the day is coming when there won't be enough work to go around, when machines will take over a good deal of the mind-destroying labours now performed by human automata, when the work week may be reduced to a few hours (or, more likely, the work year to a few weeks), when leisure may become a way of life, in its own way as difficult to cope with as some work – in spite of all these signs and portents a kind of luncheon-club Greek chorus continues to equate "work" with all that is fine and noble and leisure (which is confused with "idleness," "free time," and "laziness") with all that is sinful and debilitating.

The party line can generally be found in the pages of *Industry*, the official voice of the Canadian Manufacturers' Association, which succinctly summed up the prevailing attitude in 1948 when it clearly equated hard work and austerity with high morality:

"The more constructive form of austerity is a readiness to put in more hours of work and to work harder in those hours. . . . If austerity is demoralizing to all except the saints, then only a toughened sinner would be demoralized by a little hard work."

This Calvinist theme has been a continuing one with the C.M.A. In 1955, *Industry* editorialized that "a leisure economy with a resultant leisure market could conceivably send the nation sliding into bankruptcy. Hobbies are fine as long as work isn't one of them." The following year, the same publication asked rhetorically: "Just how much leisure can the ordinary individual use intelligently? . . . The thought of a pretty fair slice of the population living to loaf is terrifying. Actually it makes a mockery of commonsense."

The C.M.A., of course, supports a system of untrammeled free enterprise and it has specifically categorized those who oppose such a system as "too lazy . . . to pursue the opportunities it presents." Yet the real weakness in the system may be that the great mass of the people are not "lazy" enough.

A similar theme is to be found in the monthly letter published by the Royal Bank of Canada. Consider these clichés culled from *The Royal Bank Letter* during the mid-1950's:

"Work is not a curse. The law 'and by the sweat of thy brow shalt thou eat bread' may be read as one of the most beneficent laws of life. It was probably because they had nothing to do that Adam and Eve became such easy victims to the tempter. . . . As every thinking man and woman would admit, work is strengthening, satisfying, and a great blessing. It is essential to human happiness. . . . There is a kind of joy and rest after work. . . . The good life is not the idle life of a beachcomber who subsists on the bounty, the left-overs, and the wrecks of others. It is a strenuous life of responsibilities. . . . One mark of a man who is determined to achieve happiness in his work is that he doesn't ask, as a preliminary to taking a job, whether the seat is soft or the building air-conditioned. He is in too much of a hurry to get busy. . . . To be fully prepared for life you must learn to work. Someone has said that idleness is the nurse of naughtiness; at any rate it is the death of progress. Life is not a thing of ease. . . ."

One is tempted to ask the editors of *Industry* and of *The Royal Bank Letter* some specific questions: What do you mean exactly by that word "work"? Do you mean the kind of work you do or the kind a ditch-digger does? What do you mean by words like "idleness," "loafing," "leisure," and "progress"? Is a monk in a cloister idle? Is a yogi a loafer? And while we're on the subject, why on earth shouldn't a man – if he seeks "progress" – seek more comfortable working conditions? Why should he be condemned, to use your own analogy, to spend the major portion of his waking life on unnecessarily hard seats in unnecessarily fetid surroundings?

The air-conditioned office and the cushioned seat are marks of status in the executive suite; with these symbols go the responsibility of making speeches to conventions, luncheon meetings, and gatherings of the clan. One wonders, sometimes, if all the speeches are typed up by the same ghostwriter. Do major executives really enjoy listening to each other repeating the same old saws? Do they believe that, if the myths are parroted often enough, they will somehow become truths?

Consider these statements, culled over the past twenty years, from the speeches of big business executives on the subject of work and leisure:

"Work harder to produce more [the Chamber of Commerce slogan for 1951] because our survival may well depend on how fast we in concert with our friends move to get the wheels of industry in highest gear. . . ." (*Frances G. Winspear, President, Canadian Chamber of Commerce*)

"One's thoughts . . . turn too easily to leisure, to holidays, to short working hours, to long weekends when we should be thinking of more and not less work. . . . If we become soft and rich and indolent, we will lose out. . . . The foundation of our national prosperity was hard work and dedication. It would take just that to keep us great." (*James S. Duncan, President, Massey-Ferguson*)

"In place of hard work and the seeking of opportunity, we now look for security and leisure without wanting to earn them. And leisure today is seldom put to use; often it means nothing better than TV's endless stupefication. . . ." (*Paul Fox, President, St. Lawrence Corporation*)

"The greatest present danger is one of mankind's greatest weaknesses – the disinclination to work. . . ." (*Edgar Andrew Collard, Editor, Montreal* Gazette)

"Let us recapture the splendid spirit of our pioneering forefathers, who by courage and hard work made this wilderness blossom like a rose. . . ." (*John Bassett Sr., Managing Director, Montreal* Gazette)

"A man will come to less harm from overworking than he will by overplaying. Loafing is not fun to the man of spirit." (*Lord Beaverbrook*)

"One may wonder whether there is a tendency not only by labour but also by management to like leisure too much, to prefer a less arduous life to one of unremitting attention to business, to be unwilling to sacrifice our relaxed hours on our golf courses, in our homes, or in our vacation environment. Do social attitudes approve an enervating, commonplace egalitarianism rather than accomplishment?" (*Neil J. McKinnon, President, Canadian Imperial Bank of Commerce*)

"It is certainly no time to be resting on our oars or discarding those ancient Canadian virtues which are just as valid in my humble view as they ever were – the virtues of thrift and hard work. It is no time for us to be lax." (*Donald Fleming, Minister of Finance*)

"Hard work and struggle built backbone and character in our parents. And the parents by denying this just right to their children in many cases produce weaklings and loafers. Many of our outstanding leaders in city and national life today are boys from the farm who learned to do a hard day's work and still find time for study. Some of our leaders are city boys who came from humble homes, yes, and some tasted poverty; but they had the guidance of Christian parents who inspired them to work and get an education and to 'give' to society not 'take' from society. . . ." (*Hiram E. McCallum, Mayor of Toronto*)

When all this jumble of fallacy, generalization, and cliché is assembled in cold print the nonsense surely becomes obvious. Yet I am willing to lay a modest wager that I can go to the nearest Canadian Club tomorrow, utter any or all of these statements in a solemn tone, pause expectantly, and get more than a smattering of enthusiastic applause. These are the slogans of our time and the fact that they are outmoded makes them no less effective.

Most of the industrialists, politicians, and editorialists who talk so glibly of "work" are only thinking of one kind of work. They mean the kind of work *they* do, *i.e.*, work that (*a*) they like and (*b*) makes money. It does not seem to occur to them that there are two other kinds of work.

First, there is the work that people do because they have to support themselves and their dependants, but which they generally hate. Much of this work is both demoralizing and mindless and some of it, happily, is being rendered unnecessary by modern technological progress. The idea that there should be more of it is truly monstrous.

Second, there is the "work" that people do for the joy of it, whether it pays or not. This runs all the way from tending your own garden to writing a poem or painting a picture you never intend to sell. This broader definition of work does not seem to be in Neil McKinnon's lexicon. When he talks of sacrificing one's relaxed hours on the golf course or home in favour of a life of "unremitting attention to business," he obviously equates human endeavour with making a profit. Anything else is "leisure" or, to use Lord Beaverbrook's word, "loafing."

For years my friend W. O. Mitchell has been wandering about the streets and fields of High River, Alberta, thinking about his work, which is creative writing. For a long time Mitchell puzzled and baffled his neighbours. "When are you going to work, Bill?" they'd ask him, and it was useless for him to try to explain that in his terms he *was* working. Work to them was a "job" and one of the problems we face in the automated world of the future is this dangerous confusion in terms.

For men without "jobs" may still be productive and creative members of society; indeed, in the future, they may be among the most productive and creative. If we manage to change our attitude toward the Gross National Product and realize that it ought to include health, brains, and creativity then we may begin to use these resources properly. Until now they have been wasted shamefully: the nation sickly because of the lack of a comprehensive medical scheme, its brainpower half used because of a university program that caters to the upper class, its creative artists stifled because of a narrow, bookkeeping attitude to what constitutes "work."

One of the basic attitudes inherent in this establishment acceptance of the work ethic is that what is good for one generation must obviously be good for the next. Both John Bassett Sr. and Donald Fleming look back wistfully over their shoulders to a Puritan past when they speak about recapturing the splendid spirit of one's forefathers or retaining the ancient Canadian virtues of thrift and hard work. As *Executive* magazine wrote of Mr. Fleming, when he departed public life in 1963: "Hard work, genuine belief in the spiritual values of Canadian society established long ago in the crude homes and hard wildernesses of Upper Canada influenced Mr. Fleming's public and private life and are reflected in [his] political career."

Alas for Mr. Fleming and his generation, the values of Huguenot pioneers are not the values of an age which can perceive, if only dimly, a future in which the mass of the people will be loosed from the shackles of drudgery – freed, in the Greek sense, "from the necessity of labour." A true age of leisure is on the horizon. It is not the second coming of Christ that we await but the second coming of Aristotle.

The attitude of the smug minority toward leisure is as confused as it is snobbish. Once again the terms have become muddied. Hiram McCallum, Lord Beaverbrook, and *Industry* all speak of loafing. Neil McKinnon talks about laziness and James Duncan of indolence. None seems to believe that some of the time spent by some of the people away from their "work," *i.e.*, the job, may be more creative than the time spent on the job; that it may, indeed, be of more value to the nation even though it is not included in the GNP.

Time and again we are given to understand that given unlimited free time people will use it foolishly or unproductively or wastefully or indolently. This is inherent in Paul Fox's remark to the annual meeting of his corporation's shareholders that "leisure today is seldom put to use; often it means nothing better than TV's endless stupefication." It was John Porter who acidly remarked in *The Vertical Mosaic* that, though TV might well be stupefying, many businessmen thought it would also be lucrative when they sought the private station licence for Toronto. Included among them was the Argus Corporation of which Mr. Fox was a director.

It has been my observation that those members of the establishment who are not involved in drudgery and whose work is for them also a hobby are over-concerned about how the "working man" (in general those who hate their work) will spend his free time. One hears again and again that he will spend too much of it in the beer parlour. It is amazing how often that remark is made by a man who has a martini in his hand.

Such arguments are not new. In 1825, when the Boston House

Carpenters were fighting for a ten-hour day, the same cant was uttered. Their employers averred that such a measure, if it became law, would have upon apprentices "an unhappy influence . . . by seducing from them that course of industry and economy of time" to which they were anxious "to inure them." As for the journey-men themselves, they would be exposed to "many temptations and improvident practices" from which they were happily secure when working from sunrise to sunset. All in all, the master carpenters said: "We fear and dread the consequences of such a measure upon the morals and well-being of society."

This sentiment was echoed eight years later in the same city by the merchants and shipowners when the ship carpenters went on strike against oppressively long hours: "The habits to be gener-ated by the indulgence of idleness in our summer mornings and afternoons will be very detrimental to [the journeymen] individu-ally and costly to the community."

A century later, when Henry Ford adopted the five-day week, the same echoes were heard:

"Mankind does not thrive on holidays. Idle hours breed mis-chief." (*James C. Martien, President, Baltimore Chamber of Commerce*)

"I regard the five-day week as an unworthy ideal. It would be an economic *faux pas* . . . undermining our social structure. So let the emphasis be turned from leisure to work for all, from rights to obligations, from agitation to education. More work and better work is a more inspiring and worthier motto than less work and more pay. . . . It is better not to trifle or tamper with God's laws." (*John E. Edgerton, President, National Association of Manufacturers*)

3. *Liquor vendors*
lying in the sun

It is my thesis that society would benefit if it could eliminate entirely the kind of pointless drudgery which serves to degrade human beings; and that the people so employed would be better off if they were given unlimited time, with pay, to do what they want: drink beer, argue in taverns, lie in the sun and stare at the clouds, get an education, work in their gardens, or write poetry. Some drudgery has been eliminated: women no longer toil in the coal mines and young children now go off to school in the mornings instead of to the factories, and society has not crumbled as the factory and coal-mine owners once predicted it would. It may be that my own experience in a Klondike mining camp was an extreme and unusual one, but the fact remains that there are millions of people on this continent who are performing foolish and humiliating tasks in which little virtue can be found.

A very high proportion of Canadians think their jobs are dull. This was borne upon me forcefully when I set out to discover, from experts, what the dreariest jobs were in Canada. The research director of a large labour union instantly replied: "Mine." So did one of the key men in the steel workers' union. An impressive number of workers also feel their jobs are completely unnecessary. In one factory six per cent thought they were doing useless jobs. The national average for Canada is one per cent, which means that 80,000 Canadians think their jobs are useless.

A good many jobs in our mechanized Canadian society simply consist of watching machines work. A machine tender in a canning factory, for example, simply watches a group of machines turn out beer cans. A month may go by before one topples off the belt. When that happens he stops the machine and starts it again. If, in the course of an hour, a can topples two or three times, he then calls someone to come and fix the machine. This is about all he does, day in and day out.

Or take the job of a horizontal punch operator with a company like Dominion Bridge. His function is to operate and make adjustments on a single horizontal punch press which punches holes in light structural material. The material has been marked by others when it reaches him, and all he needs to do is to line it up for the proper punching procedure and then turn on the machine by means of a foot treadle. He does this over and over again day in and day out and the scene conjured up here is Chaplinesque. In one punch press arrangement, the operator must reach with his right hand over his left shoulder in such a way that he twists his body with each movement of the punch. After eight hours of this both mind and body become mis-shapen.

Surely the dullest job in the world is that of boiler watcher in a steel plant. His job is to look at the boiler gauges about once every fifty minutes. It is the sort of job that could be automated but it's considered to be cheaper to have a man on duty for the one time in six months when he may be needed. To make him feel better the boiler watcher is called a "stationary engineer."

In a mechanized society there are tens of thousands of such button pushers and machine watchers. When true automation comes they will not be needed, but unless we abandon the work ethic of another era, their lives may still be wasted because of our blind insistence that everyone must have a "job" even if the job is useless.

Such jobs exist today. Consider, for instance, the government's use of old age pensioners on automatic elevators in public buildings. There is nothing for these people to do except to stand all day while the elevator moves up and down. The elevators work just as easily without attendants and every passenger is perfectly capable of pushing his own button. Would it not be better, then, if the elevator operators were paid to stay home? Or consider the use of conductors in automatic subways. We are told by the trade press that "to relieve total boredom, the conductor is allowed to press two buttons after each stop; one to close the doors and the second to start the automatic program to guide the train to the next station." But this procedure is in no sense necessary. The conductor is as obsolete as a fireman on a diesel train. Why not pay both of them the same salary to go back to school? The economy obviously could stand it since we are paying them anyway to perform utterly useless tasks.

Let us take the milder example of a liquor store clerk, say at an Ontario Government Liquor Store. What luncheon-club speaker cares to praise the pioneer virtues inherent in this particular task? All day long our man stands behind a counter, takes a little slip of paper, stamps it with a rubber stamp, goes to a prescribed bin, produces a bottle, wraps it in brown paper, puts it in a bag, hands it to a customer, and then repeats the entire process with the next man in line. This job can be said to be obsolete. If you can get soda pop, hot soup, cocoa, chocolate bars, and cigarettes out of a machine you ought to be able to get a bottle of booze. Only the deadening lead weight of the *status quo*, plus the exigencies of political patronage, has conspired against automated liquor stores.

But suppose an automatic liquor store came into business and the vendors no longer had to spend eight hours each day in the mindless charade of stamping bin slips and wrapping bottles? Suppose their employer, the government, said: "There's only a little work left to do now so we will divide it up. Each of you will now work one month a year, filling up the machine with bottles and keeping it oiled. Naturally you'll get the same pay, since you must live, but the rest of the year is yours." For this, in effect, is what is likely to happen at some time in the future to all clerks and copy typists, carton stitchers and flanger tenders, point drivers, machine operators and button pushers of various kinds. It won't happen quite so suddenly or quite so simply, but happen it must.

Suppose this took place then. Would society be worse off if *all* of them lay on their backs and stared at the clouds, or if all of them spent their days drinking beer in the taverns or coffee in the coffee houses arguing about religion and politics? The very idea is abhorrent to us, since, being Puritans, we cannot stomach the sinfulness of it. Yet we revere as heroes and even saints men and women from the past who seem to have done these very things. When we read of religious leaders "meditating" it does not occur to us that they were doing – or appeared to be doing – the very things that the luncheon speakers decry; to wit, "nothing."

Setting aside the fact that people who stare at the clouds sometimes become poets and mystics and that people who argue in coffee houses sometimes become political leaders, revolutionaries, and social critics, it is possible, I think, to suggest that not all the liquor store employees when freed from the drudgery and ennui of their retail task would spend their time in this manner. No doubt a good many would simply watch television and go to the films; but some would travel, others would tend their gardens, read books, or improve their education. A few, I suspect, would produce something creative and thus add to the new Gross National Product of the country. But all of this would depend on a revolution in attitudes. At the moment, the evidence suggests that if all the liquor store clerks were released for eleven months of the year, most of them would try to get another job.

4.   *Did the Greeks engage in moonlighting?*

On this continent, at least, work even when dreary is comforting in the sense that it is familiar. People are not psychologically attuned to leisure. A minister I know tells me that large numbers of men in his congregation engage in meaningless activities in the church's men's groups simply because they want to get out of the house and escape the boredom. In 1955 a Gallup Poll showed that almost one-third of all Canadians believed that work was necessary in order to avoid insufferable boredom. The same conviction is apparently held by the former mayor of Toronto, in the speech quoted earlier, in which he confuses leisure with something called "play." He told his radio listeners that play carried to extremes becomes tiresome. Shortly after this he was made General Manager of the Canadian National Exhibition which is devoted largely to play. But "play" has a sinful connotation, which may be why the Puritans adopted "recreation" after the industrial revolution, a concept that makes work out of play or, at the very least, sees a man's non-working hours employed usefully to refresh or re-create him for more efficient productivity.

The idea that non-working time may be deadly and monotonous is deeply engrained in us. The Canadian Chamber of Commerce used that argument in its attack on the shorter work week in 1953:

The present drive for a thirty-hour week carries certain hidden implications. If a man works thirty hours a week and spends ten and a half hours at his meals, seven and a half hours travelling to and from his job, he is left sixty-four hours a week to fill in. For the most part people will look upon this time as leisure and look for ways and means of deadening the boredom – which means an increase in those doing non-productive work.

This establishment attitude to leisure as something that is both boring and devitalizing is a relatively new one and it comes, ironically, at a time when jobs are growing increasingly boring. Past civilizations have not valued work as ours does. The Greeks and the Romans considered work to be drudgery suitable for slaves; a man who did no work was "free." Among the Hebrews work was considered a punishment. The New Testament instruction to consider the lilies of the field who neither sowed nor reaped was the basis for the early Christian attitude toward work which carried on throughout the Middle Ages.

The eight-hour day was common in mediaeval times, and legend attributed to Alfred the Great the saying that "eight hours of work, eight hours sleep, and eight hours play makes a just and healthy day." The idea of working to make more money than one could possibly spend was a contemptible one to mediaeval man. He would, Weber tells us, find it "explicable only as the product of a perverse instinct that anyone should be able to make it the sole purpose of his life work to sink into the grave weighed down with a great material load of money and goods." Given a choice between more money and more time off, pre-capitalist man chose free time which he considered more valuable than money. The number of holidays enjoyed in ancient times is bewildering to our work-oriented eyes. Sebastian de Grazia tells us that in the so-called Dark Ages there were 115 holidays plus the inviolable

Sunday – a total of 167 days in all. In ancient Rome working days and holidays went in the ratio of two to one. In Greece at the end of the first century B.C., there were more holidays and *fête* days than there were working days. By the fourth century A.D., the Romans enjoyed as many as 175 games days (which were holidays for all) every year.

In his book, *Of Time, Work and Leisure*, de Grazia has argued brilliantly that the gains in so-called "free time" since 1850 have been largely illusory. The actual work week, he says, is not as short as statistics appear to show since part-time workers are included in these statistics. When you add moonlighting, increased time travelling to the job, do-it-yourself and housework, shopping and other activities, most of the free time vanishes.

It certainly appears to be true that because work is valued so highly today in North America people who find themselves with free time quite often drift back into old work-oriented patterns. A famous example is that of the 35,000 unionized men and women in the rubber industry in Akron, Ohio, who gained a six-hour day during the Depression. The experience in Akron suggests that – far from frequenting taverns or lying in the sun – the rubber workers did not know how to make use of their free time. Between sixteen and twenty per cent of them now hold down two full-time jobs, some of them working a seventy-two hour week. Another forty per cent have taken part-time jobs. As Daniel Seligman noted more than a decade ago in *Fortune*, "In an industry whose average hourly rate is over two dollars and which therefore leaves none of its employees impoverished, this frantic extra work suggests a rather startling value judgement between leisure and income."

Moonlighting, as we all know, is not confined to rubber workers. Clarence Long, a Professor at Johns Hopkins, pointed out in 1960 that people who do a lot of moonlighting are college professors and highschool teachers who have, nominally at least, a very short work week. The number of moonlighters in the United States is now well over three million and the number seems to be increasing. Between 1950 and 1959 it jumped by more than a million.

In May, 1957, a survey by Opinion Research Corp. suggested that fifty-six per cent of a sample of factory workers preferred the present work week with higher pay to a shorter work week with the same pay. This attitude is reflected in the fact that the major unions have not been pressing for a shorter work week for the past decade. When Premier W. A. C. Bennett of British Columbia, late in 1966, tried to cut out overtime in the Peace River Power Project and restrict workers to a straight forty-four hour week, some twelve hundred men – forty per cent of the labour force – left the job. Many of them had been working sixty hours a week. Undoubtedly the money – as much as a thousand dollars a month in pay and overtime – was an attraction. But there was a time in history when it would not have been.

The idea that leisure, not work, is impoverishing to the human spirit is deeply engrained. An Elmo Roper Poll once asked a national sample of Americans what the general over-all effect of a four-day or a three-day week would be. Twenty per cent said that people would get soft and lazy with all that leisure time; another twenty per cent said that people would get bored having so little to do. Only twenty-four per cent thought people would enjoy themselves, relax more, and be happier.

Statistics show that, in the post-war period, workers have preferred, more and more, to take a bigger slice of productivity growth in actual income and less and less in increased free time. In 1954, *Fortune* estimated that the split during the previous twenty-five years had been about sixty-forty, sixty per cent for increased income and forty per cent for more free time. But even as *Fortune* was putting these statistics together, as Einar Hardin has shown, the split had changed to the point where workers were taking eighty-five per cent of the actual increase in weekly income and a mere fifteen per cent in free time.

In a recent sample taken among automobile workers, who were questioned about how they'd use extra time off, only 16.8 per cent said they'd take another job. But a staggering 96.8 per cent said they'd spend the time "working around the house." Whether they actually would or not is another question, but it's significant that this activity – one which does use the word "work" – is listed above all others: travel, fishing, hunting, hobbies, sports, reading, going to school, resting, relaxing, joining clubs, and so on. It suggests that "free time" in North America is not equated with "leisure." The idea that conversation, for instance, might be an acceptable free-time activity is foreign to an industrial society. The idea that contemplation, in the Greek sense, might be a way of filling free hours, is simply appalling.

None of us raised in a work society, especially those of us raised before World War I, can ever quite escape the work ethic, no matter what we may believe about it, and that certainly includes the present author. In the course of writing this book, I had to consider my own attitudes toward work, drudgery, leisure, and contemplation and ask myself how they squared with my own activities:

SELF: Why do you work?

ME: I suppose to support my family.

SELF: But you make more than you spend, so that can't be the only reason.

ME: Well, I have to think of the future: the children's education, the possibility of a long illness or accident.

SELF: But you've already got enough insurance and savings to handle that. Yet you're working harder than ever before. Why?

ME: I don't call it work. What I do I enjoy. It's challenging, creative, and fascinating. It's not really work at all in the sense that the mining camp was; it's more like a hobby.

SELF: Your work is your hobby and your hobby is your work?

ME: Right. It's impossible to tell where the line is.

SELF: But isn't there *some* work you do, on occasion, that you don't find particularly creative or interesting – that you regard as a chore?

ME: I suppose so. On occasion.

SELF: Then why do you do it?

ME: I suppose if I'm offered a large enough amount of money, I tackle it.

SELF: But you don't need the money.

ME: No. Not really. Still – it's very hard to turn down a good offer.

SELF: Why? By doing these irksome chores aren't you also

turning down several hours that might be spent pic-
nicking with your children or lying in the shade talking
with your friends or walking in the forest enjoying
nature or, even, doing something else in your own line
which, while unprofitable, might be more creative?
Why don't you do that?

ME: I suppose I'd feel guilty if I shirked work to do these
things.

SELF: A-*ha!* We're talking about "work" now, and not
hobbies, aren't we? And we're talking of guilt, too.
Tell me: you say you love your work; but do you love
your work twenty-four hours a day? Aren't there times
– a Sunday afternoon, say – when crouched over that
typewriter of yours, you get the feeling that you'd just
like to quit for the rest of the day and lie around?

ME: Oh, yes. That happens to all of us.

SELF: Well, why don't you do it? You're your own boss. On
days when you *don't* like what you're doing, why don't
you do something you like?

ME: I suppose I feel I have a responsibility. . . .

SELF: To whom?

ME: To myself, I guess. If I don't finish my work when I
plan to, I feel. . . .

SELF: Guilty?

ME: Yes, dammit, guilty.

SELF: Tell me: when you *do* relax what do you like to do
best?

ME: I like to drink and talk with my friends.

SELF: How about just talking without drinking?

ME: It probably wouldn't be as much fun.

SELF: Why not?

ME: Well, in my kind of work, I can't operate when I'm
drinking. So once I start drinking I *know* I can't work.

SELF: So drinking gives you an excuse to stop working.

ME: Yes.

SELF: And you don't feel guilty?

ME: Not at the time. At the time I don't give a damn.
Maybe later on I feel guilty.

SELF: So here we are back once again to the question of guilt.
          Why should you feel guilty about using your leisure
          any damn way you please?

Why indeed? Those of us who were raised in the Depression or, as
Gordon Sinclair was, in poor circumstances at the century's turn
will know the answers. The hymns in church about "Work for the
Night is Coming" . . . the admonitions of our schoolteachers that
if we didn't apply ourselves we wouldn't get a job . . . the examples
of the adult world around us. Study was not called study, it was
called *work*. Home study was home*work*. "Lazy" was the most
over-emphasized adjective at school. Poor students were "lazy
students." Truants were lazy. I remember once during a study
period a group of us who had finished early went outside for a
round of baseball. The principal was furious; he said we were lazy
(when, really, we were just fast); we would never amount to
anything.

These things conditioned all of us, as did the Depression. To
those of us raised in that period, work tends to be more than a
means to the good life; it becomes an end in itself. And "work" by
our definition is something you do for money whether you enjoy it
or not; we cannot escape this subconscious attitude. The inse-
curities of that age remain with us in these affluent times; we are
never sure that we have accumulated enough to stave off disaster;
we cannot accept leisure because we are not conditioned to it or
educated for it. We are condemned to work . . . work . . . work . . .
and those of us who genuinely enjoy our work can count ourselves blessed.

5. *Allan Lamport meets the hippies*

Surely the strangest and most frustrating encounter in 1967 was the one that took place in the Toronto City Hall on a hot August afternoon between Allan Lamport, a city controller, and a group of hippies from Yorkville Village, the turned-on community in the heart of the town. Lamport, a man who believes implicitly that society must be organized and disciplined, and who has said that "there is no way, there must be no way that you can survive in society without working," had invited the group to come to the City Hall because he honestly wanted to understand them. But he could not even communicate with them for the hippie way of life is so far removed from the Lamport ethic as to be incomprehensible. The two groups – the hippies on one side with their bare feet (flowers between the toes) and their love signs and their exotic and brightly coloured garb; and the city fathers on the other in their dark, well-pressed suits – quickly discovered that they could not understand one another's language.

The hippies talked about "opting out" of a society where jobs had become meaningless and uncreative, where money had become an end instead of a means, where values had become distorted and love was a dirty word. Mr. Lamport and his fellow controller Fred Beavis kept talking about the need to wash, about the importance of getting a job, and about "community responsibility." The reports of the encounter read like a piece out of a play and I have so rendered it. The speeches have occasionally been condensed and paraphrased, but this is pretty well how it was in the City Hall that August day:

LAMPORT: What do you want – recreational facilities, educational facilities? What are your aims and objectives?
           (*Groans from the hippies*)
HIPPIE SPOKESMAN BLUES CHAPMAN: We don't need facilities. I don't think anyone thinks it's a crime to sit there [in Yorkville] and talk to someone.

LAMPORT: But what is it that makes you not want to be a productive member of society?

CHAPMAN: That's the very attitude I resent.

LAMPORT: (*A bit testily*) Now I'm prepared to accept your attitude no matter how invalid it may be, and I'll ask you to accept mine no matter how invalid it may be.

CHAPMAN: I don't think that's anything you have control over. We're fed up with a social system that puts the stress on production and money and places individuals in pigeon-holes, when the most important things are people's dignity and pride.

LAMPORT: A number of them haven't been washed for weeks. Now they're not seeking dignity, are they?

CHAPMAN: What's cleanliness got to do with dignity?

CONTROLLER BEAVIS: What's your objective in life? Where are you going?

CHAPMAN: My object is to engage in something that would effect some sort of change . . . to try and find a way that would give us a more effective way of life.

BEAVIS: But what *is* a hippie way of life?

CHAPMAN: Dropping out of society for a way of life that means more to them.

ALDERMAN DAVID ROTENBERG: If you want to be allowed to live your sort of life your way then you have to adjust and let older people, your neighbours, live the way they want to. The city has been receiving complaints about noisy parties, motorcycles, and couples going into people's backyards and doing what comes naturally (*he pauses*) . . . *and on private property.*

CHAPMAN: Is it all right on public property?

HIPPIE DAVID DEPOE: Most of that comes from outsiders – tourists who come down to the village to look at us.

LAMPORT: But why don't these people want to work? Because the greatest happiness in life is derived from working! (*More groans from the hippies*)

LAMPORT: I don't say it's a crime to work if you can't work. (*Laughter from the hippies*)

LAMPORT: (*Pleading*) Will you please tell us what we can do?

VOICE FROM THE REAR: Practise leaving us alone!
LAMPORT: That's nice but society doesn't work that way.
SAME VOICE: Well, what do *you* want for Yorkville?
LAMPORT: I'd like Yorkville to grow up as a shopping centre.
  (*Hoots and guffaws from the hippies*)
LAMPORT: (*Hastily*) . . . and as a place for artists to display their work and coffee houses to operate. (*Defensively*) It's to be desired. It gets a lot of tourists.

Is there a more dramatic example than this of the conflict that bedevils our time? There was a day – it seems a century ago, now! – when a younger Allan Lamport fought the Puritans and won on the subject of the Lord's Day blue laws. Because of him Toronto became the first Protestant city in Canada to enjoy professional sports on Sunday. But Lamport's iconoclasm, like Gordon Sinclair's, dies away when faced with those who would smash the real idols. He cannot stomach the terrible vision of the barefoot hippies sauntering about Yorkville, engaged in nothing more productive than conversation with their friends. Surely they must need *something*: "recreational facilities," perhaps, and one can see the vision appear as a balloon over Lamport's head: well scrubbed, crew-cut hippies in clean, pressed shorts vigorously attacking the parallel bars or leaping about on the tennis court. When the hippies guffaw, he is genuinely baffled. "The greatest happiness in life is derived from working!" He states it not as an opinion but as a truth engraved on adamant. People who oppose such a principle are dangerous to society; to stamp them out is a moral act. That is why a few days later Lamport, the usually canny politician, utters a ludicrous statement about driving all the hippies out of Toronto.

On every level the hippie movement challenges the Puritan ethic, and this is why it has caught the fancy and aroused the fury of society as no other subculture has. The Lost Generation . . . "the flaming youth" . . . the beatniks . . . the New Left – none of these movements has received the fantastic attention lavished on this small but exotic minority of young men and women. Society is as utterly fascinated by the hippies as it is repelled by them because the movement is totally foreign to our culture.

Consider the contrast between the ethics:

PERSONAL ORNAMENT: The hippies are purposeful and individual-istic in their ostentation. They wear everything and nothing. They paint their bodies and their faces as the Iroquois once did. They garb themselves in strange robes. They leave their feet bare. They go naked. They wear curious headgear. They cover themselves with bangles, beads, rings, bells; necklaces and flowers be-deck them. The dark, sober business dress of the Puritan is not for them, nor is the conformity of the uniform; no hippie dresses like any other hippie.

SENSUALITY: The hippie is totally sensuous. His dress and his en-vironment pulsate with colour. Music, light, and mo-tion are part of his world. Strange exotic sounds attract him. He delights in the tinkle of Indian elephant bells and the twang of the sitar. Incense perfumes his pad. When he dances lights flash. He revels in the joy of living. Sex is to be enjoyed freely. Drugs like LSD and marijuana are part of life. In this, as in other aspects of his philosophy, the hippie is more Oriental than Western.

WORK: The hippie rejects work in the sense of "job." He is pre-pared to work creatively – to paint, to write poetry, to act, to write for the underground press, to organize love-ins. He is not prepared to punch clocks or to engage in any task he feels to be meaningless. These jobs he calls "drag jobs" and he is only prepared to take them on as a means to an end. For him they can never be an end in themselves.

MONEY: The hippie rejects material things. If he has extra money he tends to give it away. He gets no personal satisfaction out of owning anything save the clothes on his back. He is quite prepared to go hungry and often does and it doesn't seem to matter to him what he eats. The hippie tends to live communally, sharing food and bed with friends of either sex. He is not ashamed to beg.

DISCIPLINE: In the Calvinist sense the hippie is undisciplined. He rejects the timetable and he has a different concept of time. He will sleep in to noon if he wishes and often spends his day wandering about apparently aimlessly, talking to his friends or just sitting and thinking. Going to jail implies no loss of status in the hippie culture – a fact that frustrates the police.

FAMILY: In the Haight-Ashbury area of San Francisco, the capital of the North American hippie movement, as many as thirty hippies live together in a single building, all of them unrelated to one another. This group may easily include several small children born in or out of wedlock and these children may have two or three "fathers." Hippies care less about the formalities of marriage than conventional society and some, at least, seem to have rejected the commonly held concept that a child is best off with one set of parents.

RELIGION: The hippie rejects organized religion but some of the exotic Eastern creeds intrigue him. Yogis, gurus, Zen Buddhists circulate on the fringes of the hippie world. Many a North American theologian has noted the parallel between the hippies and the early Christians: the communal life, the continuing emphasis on love, the rejection of material things, and the absolute tolerance of others. The hippie believes in leaving people alone. There is an even greater parallel between early Christianity and the sub-group within the hippies who call themselves Diggers and work unselfishly without reward to feed, clothe, house, and give legal defence to others. The hippie movement, based as it is to a large extent on psychedelic drugs, is deeply mystic, but it cannot be said to be mystic in the traditionally religious sense. The hippie may have experienced his own Heaven and Hell through LSD but he follows no divinity and he lives for the world not for the afterlife.

No wonder then that the Representatives of the People are by turns terrified of and baffled by the hippies. No wonder Toronto councilmen urge that Yorkville Village be razed, that hippies be sent to work camps, that compulsory Sunday schools be installed in hippie-land. All of these proposals are impractical in a democratic society and unworkable anyway, but their very extremism suggests the degree of panic that this relatively small group of young people has engendered.

What is it about the hippies that rattles society? It is certainly not the bright colours, the flowers, the flashing strobe lights, the acid-rock music. The adult world has already stolen these things from the hippies. Plump matrons wear hippie-like bangles and wiggle to a hippie beat. Every department store revels today in hippie colours. At Expo '67 a major theme pavilion, "Man and the Community," used psychedelic techniques to get its storyline across. The Beatles, those grand old men of the hippie movement, have the O.B.E. and the squarest of radio stations have succumbed to their music.

Is it then the hippie rejection of religion or the casual attitude to sex? I think not. On these matters the community remains divided but the division is a respectable one. Many a clergyman has expressed remarkably hippie-like views in these areas, of late.

No. The panic over the hippies goes deeper than this, and the clue to it lies in Allan Lamport's words that "these people are out to wreck society" – a curiously positive attitude to ascribe to a group that has virtually no organization, very little overt purpose, and a genuine tolerance of others. And yet, if the hippie movement spreads, society as we know it will be revolutionized, and those who support the work ethic sense it. The hippies in their rejection of the timetable and the clock represent everything the establishment has been preaching against. Their real blasphemy is that they do not believe in the virtue of work for work's sake.

Will they wreck society or save it? "The only hope for society is us," a group of them told me recently. And this may well be true. For, if the day is coming as many predict when there will no longer be enough work to go around then society will have to embrace something resembling the hippie philosophy if it is to survive. When the world ceases to be preoccupied with work, it must then face up to the very real problem of leisure.

6. *The fallacy of "free time"*

It is significant, as Sebastian de Grazia points out, that the word "leisure" should have suddenly assumed such importance in a society still worshipping at the altar of work. Newspapers have sections entirely devoted to something they call "leisure." Magazines have sprung up extolling leisure. We hear of "leisure-time activities" (surely a confusion of terms). Some houses have "leisure rooms" and there are certainly leisure clothes, leisure equipment, and leisure spending on leisure goods.

The idea of leisure, however confused it may be, has begun to have an appeal. De Grazia contends, indeed, that only the white-collar workers and the executive class have really embraced the work ethic; among the blue-collar workers, even though they have been the victims of it, it has had much less appeal. My own experience in the mining camp tends to confirm this; each year one or two men in the camp were socially ostracized by their fellows because they were "high-ballers," *i.e.*, they worked *too* hard. The rest of us had various subtle ways of maintaining the work load at a bearable pace, and some men were past masters of the art of looking busy while actually doing very little. We bore our work as a burden but we did not glory in it. The idea of work for work's sake remains an establishment concept, and the war between the establishment and the worker can be sensed in the grudging and derisive attitude to such things as coffee breaks which appear in the official publications of big business.

Nonetheless leisure remains an elusive concept and the word itself is consistently misused. Generally, it is confused with "free time," meaning time away from the job; but this time is not really free. Much of it is taken up with necessary tasks: bodily functions and ablutions, travel to and from work, shopping, prescribed visits to relatives, work around the house, sleep, and so forth. Is the rest of the free time devoted to true leisure? Not generally. Working at play remains a North American characteristic, and the goal of sports and games no longer appears to be joy but simply another method of measuring success. The active use of free time mitigates against true leisure. Among economists free time is viewed as "consumption time" just as work time is viewed as "production time." As John Farina says, in the master's thesis referred to earlier: "This non-work time is viewed in terms of its potential for creating more work rather than as a time for self-realization. The extensive consumption potential of non-work time has been expertly exploited by the disposal experts of producers and has been documented with 'work-like' efficiency."

And yet free time – time away from a formal job – is going to increase radically in the future, to an extent where if "time hangs heavy on the hands," to quote a familiar phrase, we may all go mad. Here is one vision of the future as seen in 1963 by a RAND Corporation computer scientist named Richard Bellman:

Industrial automation has reached the point of no return; the pace will increase astronomically in the next decade.

The scientific know-how to almost completely automate American industry is already available and is certain to be used.

Right now the banks could cut their staff in half easily by further automation and the steel and automotive industries, for example, could increase their degree of automation a hundredfold.

Lower and middle management will be replaced as well as production employees, for there will no longer be a need for decision-making at that level.

Jobs that are the by-product of automation will be relatively few and they will be at vastly lowered levels of interest.

A mere two per cent of the population – by implication the two per cent at the upper administrative and executive levels – will be able to produce all of the manufactured goods needed to feed, clothe, and run our society.

Within the foreseeable future, the big reward in life will be to be allowed to work.

A society in which two per cent of the people do all the work, or, conversely, in which all the people work only two per cent of the time, cannot exist on the ethic of today. Nor does the figure have to be as small as two per cent for today's attitudes to become obsolete.

It is clear that in such a society people must be paid for not working. Or, to put it another way, all those things which we lump under the term "welfare" will be vastly increased and people will have them as a right rather than as a dole or a charity.

But if people have nothing to do, won't they go crazy? Won't they die early as some executives do when they retire and find that life is empty for them? These are the questions of a society which has developed a rationale for work and recreation but no rationale for leisure.

It is observable that the hippies appear to "do" nothing and yet they do not go mad. To the contrary, they seem at peace with the world; certainly with them, joy is unconfined. Nor did the Greeks go mad with nothing to "do," nor the Polynesians.

What is needed, surely, is a change of attitude. One must return to the Aristotelian definition of leisure as the freedom from the necessity of labour, by which he meant the necessity of being occupied at any task which you had to perform but didn't want to. Leisure has nothing to do with time; it is a state; and the idea of "using" time is foreign to the idea of leisure.

We come back, then, to freedom. Leisure equals freedom. A society that truly values freedom must also truly value leisure. Leisure also connotes cultural and intellectual activity as well as community service. (In Greek times almost everybody played the flute or the lyre.) John Farina argues that the really free men of our time are the educated men of leisure: the Vincent Masseys, the Winston Churchills, the John Kennedys. They are free because they are free to make a choice, unfettered by want, ignorance, or the narrow prison of the "job."

Is it too much to expect that in the New Democracy of the future this kind of free choice will be available to all?

Publishers Urge Ottawa
End Interference with Press

The Canadian Publishers Association yesterday at its annual convention asked Ottawa to rescind second class mailing privileges to newspapers and magazines on the ground that such tax-supported largesse is an invasion of freedom.

In a brief to Parliament, the Association said that "as government expands its operations in the field of social welfare, as the tax burden becomes more crushing, as more and more Canadians look to government for assistance in a variety of ways, the will to resist such government largesse becomes weaker and weaker."

Second and third class mailing privileges were still another example of government encroachment in the free enterprise field, the publishers declared. Such interference in a free society was intolerable, the brief said.

"One adverse effect of this government welfare program is that it weakens the individual publication's responsibility for its own well-being," the brief continued, adding that such dependence on government welfare might easily destroy the character of a newspaper or magazine.

Certain struggling publications might get government aid, the publishers pointed out, if they could prove real need; but it was foolish and wasteful to carry out an expensive subsidy program for all newspapers and magazines regardless of their profit position.

200 Found-ins Charged As Police Raid Wild Party

Edward Plunkett Forsythe, well-known local industrialist and financier, was jailed last night together with some 200 guests following a police raid under Section 89 of the Liquor Control Act of Ontario.

The raid took place in the course of a wedding reception at Mr. Forsythe's palatial Bayview Ave. mansion at which, police charge, large quantities of liquor were served and consumed.

Mr. Forsythe had just finished toasting the bride, Mrs. Gerard deLacey Strathearne (*née* Coutts-Stanleigh), when members of the morality squad arrived. The bride, Mr. Forsythe's niece, is the daughter of the Hon. H. B. Coutts-Stanleigh, minister without portfolio in the Ontario cabinet.

Police charged that Mr. Forsythe had contravened subsection (*a*) of the act by permitting drunkenness in his domicile and also subsection (*b*) by permitting several of his guests, who appeared to be under the influence of liquor, to consume spirituous beverages.

Guests were charged as found-ins and transported to No. 4 police station and thence to the Don Jail where they were stripped, searched for narcotics, de-loused, and lodged in the cells pending arraignment before a magistrate.

(*Further details in the Society section*)

C.M.A. CHIEF DELIVERS BLISTERING ATTACK ON GOVERNMENT HAND-OUTS

In a stirring address to the annual meeting of the Canadian Manufacturers' Association, incoming president Weldon R. Gristle charged that government "hand-outs" in the form of new expressways were killing individual initiative and threatening basic freedoms.

Pointing out that the concept of tax-supported roads was in itself socialistic, Mr. Gristle charged that the general public was being spoon-fed by such "treats" as four-lane, no-access roads between major cities.

"Don't get me wrong," he told his listeners. "I don't want to turn the clock back and I'm not suggesting some form of vehicular artery isn't necessary. The real question is: Where will it all stop? How much can we afford?"

"Nobody is going to argue against a modest laneway," Mr. Gristle explained. "But these holus-bolus hand-outs distributed to the auto driver do nothing for the character and independence of our people.

"Surely in the final analysis it is the responsibility of the individual to find his own methods of getting to work. This consistent coddling by big government kills incentive. After all, our ancestors chopped their own roads out of the wilderness. We ought to learn to do these things for ourselves without government interference."

"Frills" in Head Office Buildings Attacked at Bank Depositors' Meet

Fancy "frills" in the new head-office building of the Imperial-Regal-Mercenary Bank of Canada came under heavy attack at the annual meeting of the Bank Depositors Protective Association today.

Speaker after speaker denounced what each terms "wild and unnecessary extravagances" in the construction and facilities for the new 65-storey edifice in downtown Montreal.

"It's time we made a true evaluation of the function of the bank and its responsibilities," Howard J. Jones, a leading depositor, declared. "Does a bank building really require a parking lot for its executives? Isn't it up to the staff to provide its own parking?"

Another speaker, Roger Rummage, revealed that several of the directors had been given private corner offices with wall-to-wall carpeting and air-conditioning. "Are these things really necessary in the day-to-day operation of a bank?" he asked. "Is it really conducive to sound business practice to flaunt these extravagances in an institution devoted to the concept of thrift?"

F. S. Carswell, who referred to himself as the bank's oldest depositor, said that it was time the bank's executive staff adopted the pioneering spirit of the bank's founders who had practised austerity for the benefit of the depositors.

"When I was a boy out West, banks were set up in shacks and tents and the interest rates were actually higher than they are today," he declared, adding that modern bank presidents were growing "soft" and "dependent."

Several depositors attacked what one termed "the extravagant expenditure" in the bank's board room. F. Scott Finch wanted to know why the board table had to be constructed of expensive African mahogany "when plain Canadian pine would serve the same purpose."

"I don't think it can be said that the banking business is in any way enriched by such 'improvements,' " one depositor remarked. "Why can't all the directors use the same washroom?"

Gavin Grableigh, Vice-President and General Manager of the bank, defended paving and landscaping of the bank's property, pointing out that it would eliminate dust, keep down malicious damage, and save depositors from injury. He added that it was impossible to secure competent bank personnel unless parking facilities and "surroundings conducive to good working efficiency were provided."

He was roundly booed by the meeting.

"There has to be a limit on spending," the Association's President, Farley Farrington, declared. "The time has come to call a halt. The depositors simply cannot afford another drop in interest rates."

Too Much Security Kills Initiative Speaker Tells Chamber

The "insatiable quest for security" among business and industrial executives came under attack from the new President of the Canadian Chamber of Commerce at the Chamber's annual convention last night in the Royal York Hotel.

An applauding audience gave a standing ovation to Kevin Waspleigh after he told them that "just as the muscles of the body atrophy through disuse, so the character of the individual is destroyed by dependence."

Mr. Waspleigh was referring to the "growing trend among many business executives and top industrialists to insist upon stock option deals, pre-paid pension plans, over-indulgent expense accounts, and other economic goodies which sap initiative."

The speaker called for a return to "the basic principles of our forefathers who built this country."

"They had faith in the future," he pointed out. "They didn't ask for fancy insurance policies to give them so-called "security" in their old age. When they went after a job they didn't inquire first if a parcel of optioned stock came along with it. They believed the future would take care of itself."

Mr. Waspleigh said that a man with a paid-up $250,000 annuity will have "less incentive to work hard to improve his economic position."

"When you remove the incentive for hard work," Mr. Waspleigh told his listeners, "you are encouraging sloth. weakness, and economic chaos."

Magistrate Orders Haircut for Musician

A self-styled musician, arraigned yesterday on a loitering charge, was ordered today to get a haircut by Magistrate F. Roger Gavel.

L. Stowkowski, who gave his occupation as "conductor," was picked up by police for loitering outside the T. Eaton Company's Christmas window. Police charged that he stared at the window for fully ten minutes, an action that tended to obstruct pedestrian traffic and contravened Section 162 of the Criminal Code of Canada.

"Are you a boy or a girl?" Magistrate Gavel asked Stowkowski, who wore a near shoulder-length mane of blond hair.

Stowkowski gave his sex as male and his occupation as conductor of the Philadelphia Symphony Orchestra.

"We've had enough of your kind lolling about the streets," the magistrate told him. "It's time an example was made."

He gave Stowkowski a ten-day suspended sentence on condition that he get his hair cut. When Stowkowski protested loudly he was fined $50 for contempt of court.

THREE **_The shackles of poverty_**

_The test of our progress is not
whether we add more to the abundance
of those who have much; it is whether
we provide enough for those who have too little._

Franklin Delano Roosevelt

1.   *The Gospel according*
      to George McCullagh

When the 1961 census was taken it was discovered that there were almost five million Canadians – four million in towns and cities and another million on farms – who were living in a state of real poverty. Of this group, at least three million were living in destitution, a condition of poverty so abject that the purchase of a ten cent newspaper becomes a luxury. These figures are almost unbelievable: in this so-called affluent society, it turns out that almost one-third of the nation is the very opposite of affluent and, by their circumstances, the very opposite of free. Few of these people can be said to be adequately clothed or housed and large numbers of them are badly fed. The proportion of sick people among them is far larger than the proportion of sick people in the general population, but the proportion of medical care they get is lower and so they stay sick longer. Most lack proper education. Though many are intrinsically intelligent and able, their potential and that of their children has been wasted by a society that refuses to invest in them. Large numbers subsist on public charity, much of it inadequate, haphazard, and unplanned.

They will always be with us, these poor, casting a blight upon society and making a mockery of our posturings about freedom and opportunity, as long as the business establishment continues to spread the myth that welfare recipients are shiftless and lazy, that poverty is their own fault, that any sustained form of government planning is totalitarian, that welfare security saps initiative, that "do-gooders" are incompetent bunglers, and that any help extended to the underprivileged should be piecemeal and minimal.

That these attitudes do exist and that they come down to us from the establishment is clear from any reading of the pronouncements of big business since World War II. For two decades there has been a consistent attempt to equate the idea of planned help for the poor with that of a slave society.

Back in 1949, the newspaper publisher, George McCullagh, a

confidant of Ontario premiers, was applauded by the Empire Club when he declared that "to sacrifice freedom and dignity for so-called security is contrary to the best in human nature. It is the way of the improvident. . . . No group of individuals constituting a nation, no matter how small or how large, can succeed with penalizing the industrious and subsidizing the lazy."

We have heard that speech many times since, and large numbers of people have accepted its several fallacies. McCullagh's economic and political power and his reputation as a social commentator rested largely upon a single action that changed his life: his ability to convince a one-time butcher's apprentice named William S. Wright to back him in his newspaper ventures with funds derived from the happy discovery of a goldmine. McCullagh was certainly industrious but his industry was of a rather special nature. He got $1,300,000 from Wright to buy *The Globe*, another $2,225,000 to buy *The Mail and Empire*, and an additional $1,600,000 to put up a new building for his newspaper. Before that time he had been a simple stock salesman, but this new alliance with Wright gave him the cachet to address luncheon clubs about "penalizing the industrious."

The proposition that anyone who accepts "security" (*i.e.*, public welfare as distinct from the largesse of gold miners) somehow sacrifices freedom and dignity was not questioned by McCullagh's listeners. It ought to be. Are the poor, the under-nourished, and the ragged actually free? Does a man who lives with his family in a tenement hovel, sharing kitchen and toilet facilities with a dozen persons, does such a man live in dignity? It is not the welfare money itself that is an affront to human dignity; it is the method of its disposal. When everyone receives the family allowance, the old age pension, or free schooling, no one is affronted. These things are taken as rights. To receive a welfare cheque one must clearly be labelled "poor." It is ironical that the very people who talk about human dignity want to keep the trunk tags on welfare recipients through a means test.

Seventeen years after McCullagh's speech about freedom and dignity, the Empire Club heard another speaker. A federal cabinet minister, Maurice Sauvé, described a typical case of poverty in Canada with such impact that McCullagh's old paper *The Globe and Mail* reported that a "ripple of unrest ran through the silent audience" as Mr. Sauvé described the case of the Carson family in Lanark County, Ontario.

Here is Mr. Sauvé in 1966 telling how Mr. Carson, a former cook but now partially paralyzed and unemployed through a series of strokes, exists with his wife and three children:

They live in an old five-room insul-brick house in poor condition. Heat is supplied by a space heater and the wood-burning kitchen stove. Water is carried into the house from an outside pump and there is no inside bath or toilet. Although they have electricity and a couple of old appliances, they have no television, radio, or telephone. They receive no papers, nor magazines, nor books. As they lack transportation and the nearest bus is thirty-five miles away, they take no part in any social organizations – even church attendance is impossible, and there is no regular local church service.

The Carsons' income is made up of the disabled persons' allowance, family allowance, and mothers' allowance and comes to about $31 per person monthly. . . . Mrs. Carson tries to supplement their living by raising a pig or two and canning food. The mothers' allowance is reduced in the summer by twenty-five dollars and she tries to make up for this fact.

Mrs. Carson is not too well. She had a medical examination following a dizzy spell last summer, but has been unable to refill the prescription which the doctor gave her. Neither Mr. nor Mrs. Carson has any teeth. They were told it was too late to get dentures even if they could pay for them. No member of the family has ever had an eye examination. None of the children was delivered by a doctor, and, with the exception of attendance by a neighbour for the actual birth of the last two children, there was no care during confinement.

Mr. Carson has a Grade IV education and Mrs. Carson completed Grade VIII. The two youngest boys attend the one-room school four miles away. Both parents want these boys to continue in school although their older brothers did not. However, the thirteen-year-old now in Grade VII intends to quit school in June.

Mr. Sauvé then went on to describe the Edmond family living in rural Quebec. The Edmonds, both of whom grew up in lumber camps, cannot read or write. They have eight children.

This family and their eight children live in a house which Mr. Edmond built in 1964. He explained that he had made it out of old planks and lumber which he found on the dump. All the family sleep in one room. There is no electricity, no telephone, no television – only a radio which doesn't work. There are four battered chairs for the ten people. There are cracks in the walls through which the cold wind blows in winter and in summer the weeds grow up through cracks in the flooring.

The Edmonds live on welfare and receive a maximum of $152 per month. This assistance barely covers essentials. Mr. Edmond used to work as a labourer in a pulp mill but since he got blood poisoning in his leg in the spring of 1963, he has been unemployed most of the time. Even when he did work, he never earned more than thirty or forty dollars a month. More and more unemployment is occurring in the woods industry. In many places, new machines have replaced many men and also it is difficult to obtain work as one grows older. Mr. Edmond is fifty-three. The two oldest Edmond boys are out of school, one sixteen and one seventeen, but they are both unemployed.

Mr. and Mrs. Edmond have little social life and recreation. They do visit with their immediate relatives occasionally. They take no part in local organizations or school affairs and seem to feel a sense of inferiority because of their lack of education. Furthermore, because of their poverty, they don't have presentable clothes to be seen in public: "We are even too poor to go to mass on Sunday – only the children go."

"There comes a time," Mr. Edmond points out, "when one gets discouraged and just doesn't know what to do. When you have no education, no money, you don't think about going to the city – there may be jobs there but we wouldn't have a chance."

These are not really extreme cases. Both these families existed on slightly less than $2,000 a year. The 1961 census reveals that there were two and a half million Canadians – apart from those living on farms – in the same economic situation. It is important to note that Mr. Sauvé felt it necessary to insist to his audience that the conditions were not the result of laziness or lack of ambition or mismanagement but lack of opportunity in a nation that has been hailed as a land of opportunity.

No wonder a ripple of unrest ran through the audience who sat beneath the crystal chandeliers of the Royal York ballroom that noon hour. So many of them had been echoing George McCullagh's words for so many years talking about "penalizing the industrious to subsidize the lazy" and mouthing pat phrases about "the way of the improvident."

---

2.   *What price Chamber of Commerce freedom?*

"One of the adverse effects of the government's welfare programs," says a booklet prepared for the Canadian Chamber of Commerce and the Canadian Life Insurance Officers' Association, "is that they tend to weaken the individual's responsibility for his own well being. The more real income and security a person gets from sources outside his own effort, the less incentive he will have to work hard to improve his own economic position." If this is true, then the inheritance tax ought to be increased to one hundred per cent. More than one-fifth of the country's business élite inherited their positions; their wealth came from "sources outside their own effort." But the Chamber of Commerce does not mean to refer to its own members in this booklet; it is referring to people like Mr. Carson, half-paralyzed in his shack, trying to raise a family of five on $155 a month.

For more than two decades, the Chamber in its role as official spokesman for Canadian business has tried to brainwash the nation with a series of statements designed to get across the Big Lie that public assistance to the underprivileged is somehow evil and totalitarian. In 1951, it gleefully applauded the president of its brother organization below the border when he attacked government welfare as "a bread and circus concept of government that leads finally to a bankruptcy of freedom and to the eclipse of human rights by the black shadow of dictatorship." The Chamber said: "The great mass of Canadians can quite easily afford life's necessities simply by cutting down on their luxury spending." This great mass does not include one-third of the nation, ridden by debt, jammed into inadequate shelter, and poorly educated by a system which conspires against the poor in favour of the rich. As for the rest of the nation, the Chamber's own members were doing their level best through advertising to force it into luxury spending.

In its bulletin for February 1955, the Chamber revealed its Calvinist side: "In the final analysis it is the responsibility of the individual to look after himself and his family. In a competitive enterprise economy, the character of the individual is made to lean upon the government. Just as the muscles of the body may atrophy through disuse, so the character of the individual is destroyed by dependence."

The Chamber, naturally, failed to draw any parallel between individuals "leaning on the government" and corporations which do the same through tariffs, subsidies, special concessions, and the kind of postal relief that allows the Chamber to mail its newsletter cheaply to its members. Nor did it consider the fact that the government protects businessmen by allowing them to employ people at poverty-established rates. For this is exactly what our inadequate minimum wage laws do; in effect, through these laws we are subsidizing employers.

In 1955 the Chamber suggested that *every welfare measure* (we must assume that here it included payments to the blind, the handicapped, and deserted mothers) was "a step toward the enlargement of state power and consequent diminution of human dignity." Eight years later it was still harping away. Once embarked on a welfare policy, it said, "it is difficult if not impossible to stop a movement toward the complete subjection of the individual by the state."

Meanwhile the Chamber had launched its "Operation Freedom" designed to make Canadians "fall in love again with freedom and to become aware of the dangers which threaten to destroy the freedom we now enjoy."

What did the Chamber mean by freedom? This paragraph from its pamphlet gives the clue: "As governments expand their operations in the field of social welfare, as the tax burden becomes more crushing, and as more and more Canadians look to government for assistance in a variety of ways, the will to resist each government largesse becomes weaker and weaker. Legislation, which controls and restricts the freedom of the individual, meets with less and less resistance."

In short the Chamber wanted freedom from taxes, freedom from the necessity of paying pensions, relief, family and mothers' allowances, and freedom from national health insurance. It was all for a return to the good old days when a handout was a handout and not a human right, and it made a man feel good all over to slip a beggar a nickel for a cup of coffee.

And what was the "legislation, which controls and restricts the freedom of the individual"? The Chamber did not say, but we may guess that it included the Combines Act which has restricted the freedom of individuals to get together in hotel rooms and arrange for identical bids on public contracts or to fix prices on everything from photo supplies and cement to bakery products and false teeth.

Did the Chamber also have in mind the restrictive and controlling legislation some of its members were pleading for in the form of tariffs, subsidies, and protections against the freedom-loving Japanese?

It is quite true, as the Chamber says, that over the decades Canadian laws have restricted certain long-cherished freedoms. The Chamber's members have been denied their freedom to hire and fire on whim, to discriminate on grounds of race or colour, or to operate machinery that is observably unsafe. These traditional freedoms have been swept away by what the Chamber calls "government interference." But the Chamber's concern "that any loss of freedom is a personal loss to each and every Canadian, and the cumulative effect will be a less-prosperous and less-free Canada" is gobbledegook.

To put Operation Freedom across, the Chamber signed up every one of its 2,700 company members, together with 850 boards of trade, using all means of communication from bulletin boards to television. Yet, large numbers of people still did not seem to understand that they were becoming slaves. Old people, for instance, who used to feel shackled in the prison of the Workhouse (a Puritan invention, be it said), kept insisting that the old age pension, though meagre, actually gave them *more* freedom. Families financially broken by unexpected medical bills had difficulty understanding how a national medical plan would somehow make them less free. Industrial workers, no longer chained to machines from dawn to dusk, continued to feel freer as the work week decreased, and some even achieved the same freedom to visit Florida that is enjoyed by the Chamber's members. Operation Freedom limped along, sagged, and was abandoned. Meanwhile, will any member of the Canadian Chamber of Commerce venture to say that the Carson family is free?

Side by side with the curious view that an all-out planned attack on the social ill of poverty somehow destroys freedom, we find two other myths being propounded.

First, there is the canard that most people receiving government assistance are parasites and that the "truly unfortunate" segment of the population is almost too small to bother about. The Canadian Manufacturers' Association in its newsletter *Industry*, for instance, has warned its readers against the kind of "loose sentimentality that will lump the many who are parasites and incompetents with the few who are truly unfortunate. Eventually these parasites living upon the strong will destroy the strong and the direction of our lives will be taken over completely by political regulation."

This simply isn't true. As of December 31, 1966, there were 970,000 Canadians receiving public funds under the government's shared-cost public assistance program. Of these, 92,000 were receiving allowances because they were blind or disabled. Are the blind and the halt parasites? Another 40,000 are confined to institutions. Are they parasites? An additional 118,000 are old people receiving old age security or old age assistance. Are the aged parasites? Another 200,000 are deserted or widowed mothers with small children, unable to work. Are these people parasites? This leaves 520,000 receiving general assistance. Of this group, 210,000 are the heads of families, the remainder are women and children. Does the

Canadian Manufacturers' Association wish to describe these women and children as parasites?

Of the 210,000 family heads, about 110,000 are disabled mentally and physically, like the half-paralyzed Mr. Carson. Are these people to be considered parasites?

This leaves about 100,000 able-bodied men, mainly seasonal and unskilled workers who qualify for short-term assistance. What has happened to the C.M.A.'s "few who are truly unfortunate"? They turn out to be an immense majority; the ratio is better than eight to one.

And are the rest really parasites? Many of them are transients with little education or skill. Some, like Mr. Edmond of Quebec, are living in an area where there is no more work. The estimates are that these 100,000 could be rendered employable, but only by retraining and relocation. But this, too, will involve government spending; this, too, will cost tax money.

Even more widespread is the generally held belief that the country cannot afford further welfare measures, which are never thought of as investments but simply as gifts. In 1959, the C.M.A.'s President, Ian F. McRae, attacked "the holus-bolus handouts distributed by Ottawa." Mr. McRae declared that "not only can we not afford this sort of thing, but such misguided prodigality does nothing for the character and independence of our people." He went on to describe the welfare-state idea as "something for nothing."

"Handouts" is the favourite word of the smug minority. *Industry*, the C.M.A. newsletter, uses it repeatedly. It implies an endless shovelling of gifts to the impoverished. "Treats" is the synonym employed by a Vice-President of Imperial Oil, Trevor Moore: "The question before Canadians today . . . do all the people who pay for the treats offered really want them or would they rather have a little more of their own money to spend for themselves? In our desire for these treats, we should not lose sight of a hidden trick, that what has been given to us will also be taken from us in one form or another."

What exactly are these "treats" that the Vice-President of an American-owned oil company tells Canadians they don't want? Do they include old age pensions, so minimal that thousands of aged people in this country must live off hot plates in single rooms? Do they include mothers' allowances, so marginal that they inhibit a full education for children whose fathers have deserted their families? Do they include welfare payments to the sick, the lame, and the blind? We do not know for Mr. Moore conveniently cloaks his brave statements in generalities. He simply refers, in this 1962 statement, to the problem of hidden taxes paying for something he calls "government services."

But when he talks about those people "who would rather have a little more of their own money to spend for themselves," Mr. Moore must be talking about those persons and corporations (including his own) who are well enough off to pay taxes; and he is implicitly suggesting – it seems to me – that they be enriched by a tax rebate made at the expense of the poorest section of the population.

There is a second inference in Mr. Moore's generalities. By the use of the word "treats" and by talking about hidden tricks of giving and taking, he is inferring that (*a*) public assistance to the poor is far too lavish and (*b*) the tax-paying public gets nothing in return for the money it spends.

Anyone who examines the facts will know that this is claptrap; but as long as the poor remain faceless these myths will persist.

3.　　　*A profile of*

　　　　the Canadian poor

Who are the poor?

The Ontario Federation of Labour defines them as "those who cannot *now* maintain a decent standard of living and whose basic needs exceed their means and resources for satisfying them." The OFL lists three degrees of poverty: first, *privation* – want of comforts of necessities of life; second, *poverty* – in want, living a subsistence level of existence; and, third, *destitution* – a condition of abject poverty.

The 1961 census revealed that 2,393,155 urban Canadians were living in conditions which can only be described as destitute. Of these, 1,862,820 were living in family groups (the average size of the family being four) whose total annual earnings did not reach the $2,000 mark. The remainder – 530,335 – were single persons living alone whose annual income was less than $1,000. There were an additional half million destitute people living "on farms"; their total family income came to less than $600 a year.

It is obvious that family income can be taken only as a rough guide to poverty, since other factors also enter into the matter. It seems to me, however, that the Ontario Federation of Labour has been conservative in its estimates. As it points out, the government itself provides a rough guide by allowing an annual income of $2,700 before levying any income tax and governments are not noted for being generous.

Besides the three million Canadians who are destitute, there are, according to the OFL estimates, two million more living in "poverty" and another two million or more living in "privation." In the first group are those urban families whose annual incomes are less than $3,000 but more than $2,000. The figure for individuals is set at $1,500 and for farm families at $1,250. In the second group are those who live in urban families earning less than $4,000 annually, or single individuals making less than $2,000 annually, or members of farm families earning less than $2,500 annually.

These cold statistics tell us that some seven million people – one third of the nation – live in a state of destitution, poverty, or privation. But statistics are faceless. Let us look at a *real* family and see how it lived in a state of privation – the upper limits of the poverty range – in the city of Toronto in 1967.

On the face of it, the Wylers do moderately well. Mr. Wyler is a truck driver, steadily employed. The family lives in a detached house, and his take-home pay for a forty-hour week in the summer of 1967 was about $70 or roughly $300 a month, which is somewhat better than the minimum wage in Ontario. The Wylers have four children, two boys and two girls, between the ages of five and ten. The Wylers budget with exceptional care and know exactly where every cent goes. Here is what they spend each month:

Mortgage payments	$ 90.00
Food	120.00
Gas (cooking)	4.00
Hydro	10.00
Phone	6.00
Auto insurance	12.00
Heat	16.00
Taxes	36.00
Clothing	7.00
Church donations	4.00
Newspapers	4.00
Gasoline, oil, car maintenance	20.00
Lunch, haircuts, personal supplies	20.00
Water	1.50
Repayment of loans from church for down payment on house	15.00
	$365.00

In addition, there is an outstanding loan to a finance company to cover the cost of the funeral of one of the Wyler babies who was stillborn, an outstanding debt to a furniture company, and an outstanding debt to a medical clinic. All in all then, the Wyler budget, which is minimal, exceeds Mr. Wyler's take-home pay by more than $75 a month. To make the extra sum he must work overtime. Sometimes he works a twelve-and-a-half-hour day and always he tries to work at least a forty-five-hour week. This, together with the family allowance, allows the Wylers to make ends meet, but just barely. They live on the edge of financial disaster. For them a single day away from work is a major tragedy; it literally means going into debt.

It is important to note the effect of the baby bonus – one of the cornerstones of the Canadian welfare state – on this family. Mrs. Wyler puts it aside carefully and uses it for dues and equipment for Brownies and Girl Guides, church girls' club, swimming lessons for the children, dry cleaning, shoe repairs, and special occasions such as Christmas and birthdays. For the Wyler children this piece of government largesse is indeed a treat and a goodie. Without it, theirs would be a grayer world.

Yet for Mrs. Wyler, a thin, careworn woman with mouse-coloured hair, life has lost most of its brightness. Like most mothers in her income bracket, she rarely goes out, living vicariously for her children. The family has had its share of bad luck. A few years ago they lost all their possessions in a fire and had to begin over again. They are trying to buy their home on the strength of a $300 down payment borrowed from their church, but the possibility of mortgage foreclosure hangs over their heads. With four children and their income, it is impossible for them to rent a flat in Toronto; yet it would be equally expensive for them to live any farther away from work. They both toil incessantly. Mr. Wyler does all the repairs on the house and on their 1956 Chrysler, and when he has any additional time he sews the children's clothes, some of which he makes himself.

In the spring of 1967 the Wylers' youngest boy was struck by an automobile. He is in hospital with serious brain damage and it will be two years before the doctors know whether or not the damage can be repaired. The car that struck him has no insurance. The Wylers do not qualify for legal aid but cannot afford a lawyer on their income. Even if they'd had free legal aid, Mr. Wyler still could not afford to take a single day off from his job to appear in court.

One terrifying incident in the Wylers' lives illustrates dramatically the fabric of the affluent society we live in. In 1966 a collection agency sent them a divisional court summons. The agency was suing the Wylers for a $274 medical bill of ten years' standing. This was a bill involving the stillbirth of a baby and it is important to point out that, though the family had a form of private medical coverage at the time, they still had to pay an additional amount.

The Wylers were now faced with a frightening situation: if the suit were successful and Mr. Wyler's wages were garnisheed, he would lose his job at once; that was the company rule. If he lost his job the chances of his getting another one were minimal: he was trained for nothing else but truck driving. Worse still, the family would lose the medical coverage that went with the job. Then what would happen to the youngest boy in hospital? The hospital had specifically asked the family to prove financial responsibility when the child was admitted, and now the collection agency was threatening, in the nastiest possible way, that he would be removed. The family managed to let the doctor know of their straits and in the end he wrote off the debt – but not before Mr. Wyler had lost almost half a week's pay traipsing about to division court and collection agency offices. This actual loss of about thirty dollars, mainly in overtime pay not received, was equal to the amount the entire family spent on food for one week.

Small wonder, then, that Mrs. Wyler appears to be on the edge of breakdown, that she cannot talk of her situation without tears in her eyes, that she winces whenever the phone rings for fear that another collection agency will be calling with more threats. Already the Wylers are slipping behind on their hydro, taxes, and Consumers' Gas bills. They are treading a financial tightrope; the slightest tremor – an unexpected sickness, more time off from work, an accident – can topple them from it, causing them to lose the home on which they have such a tenuous hold and, worse still, to face the prospect they dread the most: to go on public welfare. Yet the Wylers are immeasurably better off than most of the seven million Canadians who live in poverty or on the borderline of poverty.

We now know, for the first time, a good deal about this poverty, thanks to two major national studies undertaken in 1965 by the Canadian Welfare Council. The first study examined in depth a sample of 290 families living in poverty (but not necessarily on government welfare) in four widely separated rural areas: Inverness County, Nova Scotia; the Western Quebec counties of Pontiac, Papineau, and Gatineau; Lanark County, Ontario; and Interlake in Manitoba. The companion study examined in depth a sample of some two hundred families living in poverty in Saint John, N.B., Montreal, Toronto, and Vancouver. Taken together these two massive reports give us a profile of the Canadian poor. The picture is not a pretty one.

In the cities, the researchers discovered, half the families lived in housing conditions described as "bad or unfit for human habitation." Only a small percentage lived in detached homes. In most cases there were more people than there were rooms. The majority of the parents had less than a Grade VIII education (the percentage ranged from fifty-one in Vancouver to eighty in Toronto), and most of them did not expect their children to achieve white-collar status in the community. About half the families interviewed suffered from a chronic health problem.

The children of these families, it is quite clear, have the cards stacked against them. Sixty-two per cent of the children, it was found, got no further than Grade X and more than·half of these had left school at Grade VIII or earlier.

Why are people poor? The answers can easily be found in these two 1965 reports. They are poor because, in this youth generation, they are too old. They are poor because, in this land of opportunity, they have not been able to get an education. They are poor because, in a nation that still bans birth control ads, they have too many children.

And they are faceless: "The poor are distinguished from the rest of the people in the areas where they live not so much by their way of life as by the fact that they live on the edge of disaster at all times. Their financial margin is so slight that they cannot meet emergencies such as unemployment or illness; and emergencies are more common because they cannot be warded off."

Are the poor lazy and shiftless? The Council's urban report found that two-thirds of them were self-supporting and even those dependent on public support had become so only as a result of some personal catastrophe – usually illness, injury, or the loss or separation of the male breadwinner.

The rural investigators discovered that among the poor the prevailing condition was not laziness but of back-breaking toil. Thus the research team in Lanark County, Ontario, reported that "exhaustion and worry are very noticeable, particularly among the women." They found that among the poor themselves "the most sympathy is directed toward those who work the hardest and can't get away." There was a yearning for more rest and more conveniences, for a chance to "get away" once in awhile, and for the children to have outside contacts.

And yet, when questioned, thirty-nine per cent of the community leaders in Interlake believed that poverty *was* the fault of the poor. These pillars of society blamed such things as misman-agement, alcohol, laziness, and lack of ambition for the appalling conditions in their midst.

But is it lack of ambition when a man recognizes the inevitabil-ity of a low-paying job when he has no training for anything else? Is it laziness that keeps poor families working long hours at hard labour? Is it mismanagement to get behind when one's income is less than one needs to feed and clothe a family? As Michael Harrington has said in *The Other America*, we do not require of cripples that they should run races. Must we make similarly out-rageous demands of the economically crippled?

---

4.   *The vicious cycle*

        of want

Who gets welfare and why? Are we ruining people with too many handouts? Have we gone overboard on welfare payments?

If the Canadian Welfare Council's surveys are valid, quite the opposite is true. In its study of rural poverty, the Council discov-ered that the real problem wasn't too much assistance; most people were caught in the trap of poverty because they weren't getting enough help to free themselves. "Inadequate welfare pay-ments may tend to contribute to maintaining poverty rather than relieving it. The Inverness study suggested that the longer a family is on welfare, the poorer they become; furniture, for instance, wears out and cannot be replaced, housing repair and mainte-nance is put off, etc." In Interlake, the ten families on welfare were leading such a submarginal existence that they "seemed defeated by circumstances. They could see no way out of their hopeless situation. . . . You had to sink very low to get assistance and when you did it was only enough to keep you there. . . ."

Then why not go out and get a job to improve yourself?

This is the question society continues to ask. The answer is that this is often not possible. The Canadian Welfare Council reported that among the rural poor receiving welfare "sickness and chronic disability were reported in a majority of cases." As we have seen, the same thing was true in the cities, where welfare payments were accepted "as a necessary but degrading experience. Having no choice, they are glad to have the aid but feel it is not enough to let them feel they can take a normal part in the community."

In Inverness County, Nova Scotia, the Council's rural investigators discovered a family we will call the McDermotts. Mr. McDermott was fifty-eight and disabled; he had twelve children all under the age of sixteen. The fourteen people were living in an old farmhouse on $90 provincial assistance and $74 family allowance: an average of $11.71 a month per person.

The McDermotts' leisure consisted of visiting neighbours and friends, attending weddings and funerals, and watching television. They could afford nothing else. For clothes they depended upon the charity of neighbours. They were not happy about being on welfare and if Mr. McDermott could work, he would. But his heart condition prevented that.

As the Council's interviewer notes, "The family is in pretty bad shape. Their income enables them only to exist. They probably would be a good family to put more money into as they seem to realize the value of it and could probably manage it well."

Yet the campaign continues to prevent extra tax money being spent to lift people like the McDermotts out of a vicious cycle of poverty. The editorial writers and popular newspaper columnists have taken up the cry. When John Turner, M.P., comes out in 1967 for a guaranteed annual wage, subsidized housing, free university education, and a medical scheme, Dennis Braithwaite in *The Globe and Mail* jumps on him with both feet. "We don't want any more handouts, thanks a lot," cries Braithwaite, a former left-winger who, long ago, turned his coat. *The Kitchener-Waterloo Record* attacks "handouts from the public treasury" declaring that "there may be a few lazy people who are sick. The majority are just lazy." *The Chatham News* hits out at "more money squandered in providing doles for non-producers." In the Thompson newspapers, Ottawa columnist Patrick Nicholson parrots a familiar line: "With every extra government crutch the individual loses a bit more of himself, of his individuality and self-reliance."

James McDermott of Inverness County, Nova Scotia, has lost his self-reliance and unless something is done his twelve children will lose theirs, thus perpetuating the cycle of poverty for which, eventually, we will all pay – the Braithwaites and the Nicholsons and all the editorial writers and their children. In the words of the Toronto Family Service Association: "Caught in the economic underground of today's poor, there is little chance for a child to escape, little to motivate him to reach out for the educational skills that he will need to compete in this automated age. Rags-to-riches is becoming more and more a rags-to-rags story." The Horatio Alger hero is dead. He was never much of a hero anyway; in a surprising number of cases he achieved success by the shortcut of marrying the boss' daughter.

The cycle of poverty is graphically illustrated by the case of a Mr. Connors, one of twenty-five case histories carefully studied by the Family Service Association in Toronto. Mr. Connors, a father of six, found at the age of forty that his income was fluctuating and unstable because of the seasonal shortage of work. He had a Grade IX education but that wasn't enough. He tried retraining but he discovered that the cost of the streetcar fare plus the fee for the course cut so deeply into his family food allowance that he couldn't continue it. This will seem unbelievable to some people, but the facts are that the Social Planning Council's Guide to Family Budgeting showed at the time that the eight-member Connors family needed $519.76 a month to live decently. In actual fact, their income totalled $265.59, including family allowances. Out of this they paid $95.25 for rent; this meant they were forced to feed everybody on a budget of about four dollars per person a week. When clothing was needed, it had to come out of the food budget. Anyone who has bought shoes for children knows the disastrous situation this family found itself in. It was caught in what the Family Service Association called "the vice of poverty."

In failing this family, society failed itself, for it is apparent that the six Connors children, no matter how high their I.Q.'s may be, can never be fully trained to make use of their resources and abilities. The great hope that Mr. Connors and his wife have is that their children will be able to "learn enough to get steady jobs some day." That is a hope that defies realization. The chance of any of them progressing very far in school is minimal. As the F.S.A. asks, rhetorically: "Suppose the lure of a new dress sends a teenage girl out to find a job? Or a sixteen-year-old boy drops out of school to help pay some medical bills?" This is exactly what is happening in the perpetuating sub-culture of the poor.

The verdict on the Connors kids: "Without proper training these children will slip into the same routine of periodic unemployment which plagues their parents."

What happens to a child whose family is forced by circumstances to exist on public welfare? The case of the Gundersons of Toronto is a good example. These are middle-aged people who look about ten years older than they really are. Mrs. Gunderson has steel-gray hair which she must wear straight back since she can never afford a hairdresser, and on her face she wears the distraught look of perpetual anxiety which is a kind of trademark with women in her situation.

James Gunderson has had no work since he injured his back on a construction job. Before that he had been truck driver, elevator operator, office cleaner, and day labourer. Now he wears a Harris brace and is not allowed to lift anything. In 1967, he was offered a job washing the walls of the subway; he could not take it because he cannot do any task that causes him to bend his body.

He, his wife, his eleven-year-old daughter, and his nine-year-old son subsisted in 1967 on monthly welfare payments of $184.30 plus the family allowance of $14. They lived in their brother's house, which was fortunate for them, since it gave them more living space than most welfare families and at a reasonable rate. After they paid their $100 in rent, they had almost $100 left over for food, clothing, hydro, and incidentals. They lived on hamburger, stew, beef bones and potatoes, and soup made from potato water. Eggs were rare in this family; roasts non-existent.

But it is not what they could buy that is significant here, it is what they *couldn't* buy. Neither child, for instance, has ever been able to buy an ice-cream cone. In this family a dime is a big sum, equal to half a loaf of cheap bread. The children have never seen a movie. Perhaps more important, the family literally cannot afford a picnic outing to a place like High Park because of the streetcar fares. It costs twenty cents each way for three adults and an additional twenty-five cents return for a child; total, $1.45. Toronto Island, that weekend mecca for the masses, is equally out of the question. Add to the $1.45, another ninety-five cents for ferry fare. Double that price in the winter. Add an extra quarter on Saturdays when children must pay full fare. These prices are exclusive of the treats that are usual on such occasions. It would be hard to handle an outing to the Island for less than $3.50, a sum that would pay half the hydro bill for the month. Perhaps with a new schedule of welfare payments in effect in 1968, the Gundersons may be able to afford such minimal luxuries. But it is callous and unthinking to suggest, as some do, that they have been treated extravagantly or even generously.

When the Gundersons' daughter, Kathy, goes to Girl Guides, she must do without a uniform since her parents cannot afford to buy one. Jamie, aged nine, is in the Cubs. His mother has managed to get him a cap, scarf, and shirt but the shorts are simply too expensive. He badly wants a pair since his friends have them but, thus far, it is out of the question. As for a bicycle, there is no hope for that.

"It breaks my heart not to give them these things. I tell them that their father doesn't work and they understand but they forget quickly," Mrs. Gunderson says. "My big worry is that they'll start to steal things." Eva Gunderson is a woman who lives as in a jail. She rarely leaves the house since her only recreation would be window shopping along Bloor Street, an activity that frustrates her because she can't buy anything. She and her husband have not seen a movie since their courting days. Neither ever buys shoes. His badly need half-soling, but the family cannot afford the three dollars this would cost – a situation that makes it even more difficult for a man seeking a job.

In 1967, Jamie Gunderson, who had been doing well at school, suddenly developed a perceptual handicap. He simply stopped learning, and it seems clear that the troubles at home contributed to the problem. Once again the curse of poverty comes full circle. Jamie's father, raised in a poor family, worked pushing a handcart at nights when he was a small boy at school. When he reached

Grade IV, school became too much for him and so he went to work full time. Jamie's mother, another product of poverty, went to work after Grade VIII. Neither parent is stupid; both could have gone much further in school. Neither is lazy, shiftless, or ne'er-do-well. Their home is spotless, their budgeting frugal, and their willingness to work unquestionable. They are doing the best they can for their children but, at this writing, the chances of young Jamie Gunderson ever fulfilling his full potential seems unlikely. Years from now our children may be paying taxes for his board and keep.

A quite different case is that of Roger Lowe, whom most people would certainly call shiftless. Lowe is a sparrow-like man, with a lined, anaemic face, who seems to subsist almost entirely on Maxwell House instant coffee which, through television, has become a kind of status symbol for him. Lowe belongs to the hard core of welfare cases in Toronto who are listed unemployable for psychological reasons. He says flatly that he doesn't want to work, doesn't intend to work, and prefers to live on welfare. He is a braggart and a know-it-all who conceals behind his bold exterior a terror of the world at large. Yet, when you study Roger Lowe's background, you begin to understand him.

He is, in the words of a social worker who knows him well, "a classic case of the unemployable." From the day of his birth he has had nothing going for him and that is equally the case of his wife, a pasty-faced woman with a forlorn and beaten look about her. In his youth, in Nova Scotia, Lowe was deprived of almost everything a child needs. His father died when he was one year old and he was forced to quit school at Grade V and go to work pushing a handcart to help out his family. He worked at various casual jobs until a few years ago. Then, for all practical purposes, he stopped. Those who have studied his case believe that his environment long ago stunted his intellect. As for his wife, she was placed in an orphanage early in life as a result of her mother's re-marriage to a stepfather who treated her with great cruelty. She quit school at Grade VI in order to go to work and she has been working to this day.

There is no hope for Roger Lowe, long since a drop-out from society. But there might be for his children. The Lowes are Roman

Catholics and they have had nine offspring, two of whom have been sent out for adoption. At the time this was written, the rest of the family – seven children and two parents – were living in a three-bedroom upstairs flat in the Cabbagetown area of Toronto subsisting on $183 public welfare (of which $100 went for rent) plus family allowances.

The interesting thing about this family is that, though their economic situation has been far from perfect, and though the male parent is outwardly a ne'er-do-well, the family is a close one and the children feel secure. They do reasonably well at school and can probably continue to do so as long as the family sticks together. But it looks as if the Lowe family is about to fly apart and for an ironical reason.

In the fall of 1966, the Lowes were told they would have to leave their present quarters and find other housing because they contravened a city by-law which says that there must be one hundred square feet of floorspace per person in multi-family dwellings. Mrs. Lowe, then pregnant with her seventh child, and the other six children were removed to an emergency housing centre established in the Richmond Street armouries. Mr. Lowe was packed off to Seaton House, a hostel for down-and-outs.

Whatever the environment had been in Cabbagetown, the emergency housing was far worse for the children. In this barrack atmosphere, with its thinly partitioned cubicles, its institutional feeding arrangements, and its minimal bathing and toilet facilities, there was nothing for the children to do save sit on their beds all day or wander in the downtown streets. (Some of the children started to play in the basement but were evicted for making too much noise.) After three days, Mr. Lowe arrived, literally kidnapped his family, and returned to the crowded Cabbagetown quarters. The city authorities let them stay there for a year, but in August of 1967 they were told they must leave. The social workers on the case firmly believed that, if this happened, the family's security as a close-knit group would come to an end, the father would vanish in frustration, the children would be separated, and the cycle of poverty would be joined for the next generation. Since there is scarcely any other place for a nine-member family living on welfare to go, it seems likely that conditions will force the permanent breakup of the Lowes, and the sins of the fathers will be visited upon yet another generation at the usual cost to society.

Poverty damages us all, the rich as well as the poor, and in the end we must foot the bill for it, albeit in a piecemeal fashion: a larger police station here, a new home for the emotionally disturbed there, more penitentiary space, increased family court facilities, expensive urban renewal schemes. It is striking how often in Canada we try to meet our problems by building something we can see. In the Centennial Year, for example, we built 145 libraries and eighty theatres, art galleries, and museums but spent precious little to subsidize the writers, painters, playwrights, and actors who in the end must make those structures come alive. We are always prepared to repair or improve something we can look at, like a road or a causeway. Indeed, we insist upon such repairs. But human repairs and improvements remain beyond our ken, and when someone suggests we initiate such a program of renovation of the human body and spirit he is reviled as a do-gooder making free with our tax dollars. We have not yet applied to our social policy the principles and techniques of rational calculation, research, innovation, and technical progress that we insist upon in our industrial system. That is "planning" and planning is evil and totalitarian. Yet, in the end, the real cost to the nation of this attitude to planning will not be in the expensive stop-gap measures we are finally forced to pay for but in the appalling wastage of human resources which we permit every time social conditions prevent one of us from attaining our full potential.

---

5. The folklore of motherhood

A striking feature of poor families, especially those on government assistance, is the high proportion which have no breadwinner.

The Canadian Welfare Council discovered, significantly, that forty per cent of the city welfare cases were families with no father present. Among the non-welfare families in the poor section, however, only six per cent were without fathers. These are revealing figures in a nation which is supposed to respect motherhood. The system as it stands conspires against the mothers among the poor: they are damned if they stay home as "parasites"; they are damned if they go to work for "neglecting their children."

Consider this situation, described to me in 1966 by a woman I shall call Mrs. Shaw, living in a small Ontario town:

"I am sixty-two years old. Ten years ago my husband and I thought we were pretty well off (and we were). We had our place all paid for, a nice car paid for, and a couple of thousand dollars in the bank. Also he had a good job with the Department of Highways.

"Just about that time our sixteen-year-old daughter was in Grade x, doing well. I had for years kept Children's Aid kids because I had a big house, not much to do, and lots of love to bestow on these little unfortunates. One little boy really took our hearts and we adopted him. Then our own son wanted to marry a girl with an illegitimate daughter and so to help them out we adopted the little girl, too. We felt we were on top of the world.

"Then, one day, our sixteen-year-old took sick. In two weeks she had been taken to the hospital in Toronto where she died of nephritis. The next year my husband died with a brain haemorrhage. Well, you can imagine me all alone with these two children. My money was gone and still I owed for my husband's funeral. Well, I boarded the children out and went to work through a home nursing agency in Toronto. I paid the funeral expense this way, but then I developed diabetes. My doctor suggested I apply for mothers' allowance, which I did. I got along until my little girl was sixteen years old. Then I went to work part time at a local nursing home. With this extra money I planned to send her to hair dressing school. But when the government discovered I was working they cut my pension way down.

"At the moment I receive $101 a month for mothers' allowance and am trying to educate my boy, now sixteen years old and in Grade xii. If my health continues, and if the mothers' allowance let me keep the pension to help me, I will see that he studies long enough to be a teacher, which is his ambition.

"My diabetic pills are $6.25 for fifty. I take two every day. I can't afford meat for myself but I always have one good meat meal every day for my boy. I sure have struggled along but – who knows? – some day I may have all I need to live on.

"Don't use my real name anywhere or I may lose my pension for talking."

Mrs. Shaw's letter tells us so much about the Canada of the Sixties – the myths we live by and the realities behind them. Her situation underlines what has been the basic Canadian attitude to welfare payments: *It is bad to give people, no matter what their circumstances, enough public assistance to allow them to live in dignity and freedom. Make sure that they receive no more than the absolute minimal standard. Give Mrs. Shaw enough so that her boy gets one meat meal a day but not enough so his mother can enjoy meat. If she earns a little extra, deduct that from her allowance – anything else would amount to a coddling of the poor.*

Though there are some changes on the horizon (Mrs. Shaw may be able to eat some meat in 1968 as a result of increased welfare payments), much of our welfare apparatus is still based on poor-law thinking because society accepts the whip-and-carrot thesis. Remove the threat of the whip, withdraw the promise of the carrot, and, so the theory runs, society will collapse. This concept was specifically challenged in June, 1967, by Robert Theobald, the British socio-economist, in an address to the special conference on Social Welfare Policy in Canada when he pointed out that modern psychological theory takes the opposite view: that man will strive for self-realization if he is provided with the means to satisfy his basic needs. The present system operates on the theory that an individual must be forced to earn his own living by making his condition so unpleasant that toil will appear more attractive. But, said Theobald, "If man is drawn to the goal of self-realization as his immediate needs are met, then the present welfare system is the *very* factor which is preventing many from realizing their own potential and contributing to the needs of society."

None of this theorizing solves the problem of Mrs. Shaw, sixty-two years old and diabetic. The frightening thing is that the act of God which changed her life could strike at anybody. Tens of thousands of women, none of them lazy or drone-like, could find themselves in the same position tomorrow. Mrs. Shaw was fortunate. She owned her own home and so could spend the entire sum of $25 a week on her children's food, clothing, and education. But was the allowance she received a "treat"? Did she, to quote an old line from Fred Gardiner, the one-time Big Daddy of Metro Toronto, "sacrifice her individual freedom for a promise of social security"? Was she one of the Chamber of Commerce's great mass of Canadians "who simply must cut down on luxury spending"?

There were, in 1966, some seventy thousand mothers in a position similar to that of Mrs. Shaw. All were the victims of a double attitude in Canada which has made life for them close to intolerable. Whether they stay home on welfare or go out into the world to support their families, they are condemned by society.

A young mother, stranded and alone with two or three small children, may very well decide not to be a "parasite" in the C.M.A. sense. Suppose then she decides to go to work to support her family? To make it worthwhile she must find a job that will pay her more than the combined total of her government allowance and the cost of child day-care. But if she dares to suggest that public funds be used to care for her children by day, while she becomes a productive member of society, she will be in for it.

For the same sort of people who urge the Puritan virtues of self-reliance upon the destitute, who want everyone to pay his or her own way, who feel that those who accept public welfare are drones – these are the first to utter a self-righteous cavil when a woman takes a job and leaves the care of her family to others. Such a woman is a second-class citizen, considered by many a menace to society and a cause for juvenile delinquency, unworthy of either sympathy or assistance.

These, at least, are the reasons publicly cited by society's spokesmen when the question of approving publicly supported day nurseries for the children of working mothers arises. As the press reported on July 5, 1966, "The majority of Ontario municipalities continue to hold out against publicly financed or publicly assisted day-care centres on the grounds that a woman's place is in the home." Thus, by invoking the myth of motherhood, do the politicians salve society's conscience while saving tax money.

"Working wives are contributing to many social problems,"

declared Louis P. Cecile, when he was Minister of Welfare for Ontario. "These women show disregard for their offspring. . . . Mothers should accept the job of fulfilling the most important role of all – that of wife and mother."

"It becomes human nature for a mother to take care of her young," said O. E. Crockford, Chairman of the Welfare Committee in the Toronto suburb of Scarborough, when, in 1965, the council was asked to make a grant to pay the salary of a social worker to supervise a co-operative day nursery in the township's public housing project.

Two other powerful municipal politicians in the Toronto metropolitan complex went even further. Miss True Davidson, the Reeve of East York (who sometimes blurts out statements she doesn't mean), opined that the suggestion that day-care nurseries be provided for all "reminds me of Russia." Not to be outdone by this reference, Reeve John Macbeth of Etobicoke said the whole thing "sounded more like Chinese Communism." "It's not my system and it's not democracy," said Reeve Macbeth. Later the Reeve said that he would rather pay a mother to stay home – "there would be less juvenile delinquency."

That society is hypocritical on the subject of working mothers is easily demonstrated. In the words of the Social Planning Council of Toronto, "Shortages of skilled personnel, such as nurses, teachers, social workers, clerical and secretarial help are often met by inducing married women to remain in the labour force or return to it, whether or not they have young children." How many businessmen who rail against working mothers have also tried to persuade a valued secretary to stay on the job, small children or no? And does Reeve Macbeth employ only spinsters?

There is a curious class distinction here which again underlines the hypocrisy that exists on the subject of day-care centres. As everyone knows, large numbers of upper-class mothers board out their children at private nurseries, private schools, and expensive summer camps. These children spend no more time in the bosoms of their families than do those who are left during the day in the handful of publicly supported centres across the country. Yet the private camp, the private nursery, and the private boarding school, far from being considered wicked, are labelled "mind-enriching" and seen as status symbols. No one, in Louis Cecile's words, charges that upper-class mothers who pack their children off to expensive institutions "show disregard for their offspring."

This kind of doublethink prevailed, I suspect, when Viola Liuzzo, the Chicago mother of five, was murdered during a civil rights demonstration in Alabama in 1965. A good many people at that time were heard to ask what business Mrs. Liuzzo had "deserting her children" to take up a cause. Yet had Mrs. Liuzzo spent the same time on vacation with her husband, leaving her children in the care of the housekeeper or relative and been killed in an auto accident, no one would have been outraged.

Whether or not a mother's place should always be in the home is a debatable question. (Four out of five mothers charged with juvenile delinquency, according to the Dominion Bureau of Statistics, are *not* working mothers.) But the realities are that, in the present state of Canadian society, thousands of mothers cannot afford to be. In 1964, there were one million children under fourteen, including 38,000 under six, whose mothers were working. These children are parked with relatives, friends, and even at work. Only two per cent, in 1964, were in group care such as day-care centres or after-school centres.

In Toronto, according to the last census figures, there were 24,000 mothers who had to work because they had no husbands. There were – and are – at least 10,000 children needing day-care. (Some schools in Toronto must now open their doors at 7.30 a.m. in order to accommodate children who have no where else to go because their mothers have left for work.) Yet all of the nurseries in town, public and private, can handle only 2,700 children. Of these nurseries only nine are tax-supported even though, since 1946, the municipalities have been able to get half the funds for such support from the province (a situation that does not exist elsewhere in Canada). The Social Planning Council has reported that unsatisfactory private placements are being made by working mothers, including some that were "actually dangerous due to overcrowded conditions, health hazards, or inadequate supervision of children.

One private day-care centre in Toronto consisted of a tiny one-bedroom apartment, in which twenty pre-school children were confined, supervised by one elderly woman. Worse still, one Toronto woman, whose own children were mortal victims of the much-discussed "battered child syndrome," was found to be running a private day-care operation. There is little doubt that publicly supported day-care centres could reduce the incidence of child neglect that continues to make newspaper headlines. But this, too, will involve tax money.

Society cannot have it both ways. If we really believe a woman's place is in the home then we must show it by abolishing poverty among those mothers who are the sole support of the family. If we can't do that then we must be prepared to pay taxes to support properly run day-care centres for the children of those we force to work. But in neither case can we honestly pretend that these payments are part of "a bread and circus concept of government."

---

6.   *Must "planning" be
        a dirty word?*

In 1961, the University of Toronto's Director of the School of Social Work, John Morgan, wrote that "the Welfare State is as out of date as the Model T."

It still is. The various welfare services in Canada are ambulance services designed to rush in at the eleventh hour and apply splints to people already badly crippled. What is needed is a plan for preventive social medicine – of which the guaranteed annual income might easily be the foundation – which will be accepted by the general public as casually as it now accepts the plans for a new post office. The advantages of such a systematic and planned attack on poverty ought to be obvious. Can we afford it? Surely the answer must be that we can no longer afford to ignore it.

Some tentative plans have been made in this direction but they have been a long time coming and they will be slow in hatching.

The very term "planning" has, after all, been a dirty word in Canada for a long time. The business establishment has purposely made it so.

Again the Chamber of Commerce has led the attack. Its bulletin has consistently hit out at those who would support a planned society. Similarly, *The Property Owner*, official voice of the Ontario Property Owners' Association, has railed against "the social planner with his unrealistic and childish attitude toward costs"; the Empire Club has applauded attacks (by a United States steel tycoon) on "the dismal effect of central planning"; and, as might be expected, *The Royal Bank Letter* has had its say. It is curious that businessmen who wouldn't erect an office complex without a set of carefully prepared architects' blueprints, who wouldn't dream of leaving their personal future unplanned through lack of insurance policies, who won't go for a two-day business trip without drawing up an itinerary – these same people are opposed to any form of planning by government.

In his 1964 study of *The Family in Canada*, Frederick Elkin reported on a group of forty-seven multi-problem families in the Ottawa area. The families were living in housing which was crowded, in poor physical condition, and costly. The education of the adults was Grade IX or below and all the families were suffering from serious financial problems. The cost to the community must have been enormous *since these families were using thirty-five different health and welfare agencies*. Elkin reports "as is not uncommon, the agencies did not co-ordinate their help to these families so each agency did not really know what the others were doing."

This lack of an overall welfare plan has worked terrible hardships on people caught, through no fault of their own, between the various agencies. In November, 1966, *The Globe and Mail* reported the case of seventy forgotten patients in Toronto nursing homes who were the victims of a horse-and-buggy welfare philosophy. The paper outlined the case of Stanley Jones, a sixty-one-year-old former truck driver, as an example.

Jones had worked hard all his life, paid taxes on three homes, and contributed for years into the Unemployment Insurance Fund. But he had suffered a kidney ailment and a paralytic stroke, and when his wife died he had gone completely to pieces. Jones' money had gone. He was a recipient of public welfare from the city. But the hospital insurance people said he wasn't sick enough for full hospitalization. Since hospital insurance doesn't pay nursing home bills this became a welfare matter, for Stanley Jones, though not sick enough for hospital, was too sick to look after himself.

Welfare therefore paid for his nursing home; but for nothing else. Jones was too young at sixty-one to qualify for a pension; therefore he was too young to have any pocket money. Along with seventy other patients in the city he had to beg if he wanted anything personal; razor blades, a haircut, cigarettes, toothpaste, a stamp for a letter, or a daily newspaper. When the Canadian Chamber of Commerce talks about planning and freedom, it ought to ask itself whether in the free and unplanned society it advocates Stanley Jones is in any sense a free man.

But to have a plan one must first have a social attitude to support it. One way to change the attitude would be to get rid of that word "welfare" and substitute some such phrase as "income maintenance." In an affluent society there ought to be an income floor under every man below which society will not allow him to go – and this ought to come as a right and not as a charity. Yet the business establishment continues to support the idea of a means test for all welfare payments, as it once supported the idea of a means test for anybody desiring free schooling.

The phrase "means test" is not used as often as it used to be. The party line has been subtly changed to avoid that uncomfortable term. It now goes like this: "Our complex social welfare program puts so much emphasis on the principle of universal benefits that much of the money goes to those who are quite capable of looking after themselves. . . . Is it not time we went back to the basic principle of helping the needy?" The quotation is from the *Daily Journal Record*, Oakville, Ontario, for July 11, 1964.

On the face of it this makes eminent sense to some people. But to help the needy only, you must label them objects of charity and this is intolerable. Having to prove need is degrading. It involves government snooping and, more than that, it freezes initiative. As the Toronto *Star* editorialized in 1967, "Why should a man try to find work when every dollar he earns over a pitifully small amount is a dollar less he gets from the state?" I know a handicapped man who cannot get the new government pension of $105 a month because he has one thousand dollars worth of liquid capital. And if he earns more than $24 a month on his own the government will take eighty per cent of the difference.

The solution that many have proposed is a guaranteed annual wage based on a negative income tax, in which income is declared as on an ordinary tax form and those who earn less than the agreed minimum – it should not be less than $3,500 – receive federal grants up to this amount.

This will be an expensive and controversial undertaking. One can hear the screams from the business community, along the lines of the address given in 1965 by the C.M.A.'s President Humphrey B. Styles. Mr. Styles, differing not one whit from a long line of predecessors, called for what he termed "hard thinking in the matter of social service priorities." He said there was a "world of distinction between a limited, common sense social security and a rampant welfarism psychology carried to the point where more and more people think in terms of being spoon-fed from the cradle to the grave." Mr. Styles then said that he, of course, didn't want to turn the clock back.

As usual, the C.M.A. was trying to convince the nation that the welfare state had gone as far as it could go or should go and that there should be no further expenditures of public money to fight poverty, provide more educational opportunities, raise present welfare payments to a realistic figure, subsidize day nurseries, or allow the aged and infirm to live in dignity and comfort.

"There is no such thing as 'free' goodies for anyone," said Mr. Styles, playing the same record once again. One wonders sometimes why C.M.A. presidents bother to write themselves a new speech. The same old speech that has been given for the past twenty years will do just as well.

There is no use pretending that the cost of eliminating want and privation and of providing equal opportunity to all in Canada will be cheap. As long as the business world talks as if such an attack was a luxury and not a necessity, a handout rather than an investment, then the public will balk at paying for it.

Oddly, few people balk at twelve-lane highways; governments

which spend the public's money on such things seem to be returned to office with clockwork regularity. But then highways, dams, seaways, expositions, airlines, railways, and expensive buildings are never presented as "treats" and "goodies" by speakers at business conventions. Stockholders never seem to question big business executives whose companies insure their lives for large sums – a form of security which is never seen to be debilitating. Nor do they stand up at annual meetings and charge that those directors who insist on wall-to-wall carpeting in the executive suite are being spoon-fed.

Anybody who gets an income tax deduction for his wife, his children, or his old mother is receiving government welfare, though no one ever calls it that. Every well-to-do businessman who enjoys a company car or a fancy tax-deductible pension scheme is getting public welfare too, though that word is never applied to people in the top income brackets. Yet the community pays for a large proportion of these goodies and treats and, as John Morgan has pointed out, "their justification is precisely the same as the justification for the old age pension."

This Chamber of Commerce attitude to welfare as a straight handout to the underprivileged was reflected in Mitchell Sharp's policy in December, 1966, in introducing a "minibudget" to cover the cost of increases of $30 a month to the poorest of the old age pensioners. In spite of the fact that ample reserves existed in the old age pension fund to cover the added costs until the spring budget came down, Mr. Sharp insisted on increasing sales and income tax just enough (he said) to pay for the higher pensions. Why? He wanted, he said, to show the people that the cost of new government programs must somehow be met.

Was it really necessary for Mr. Sharp to demonstrate how much the undeserving poor among the pensioners were costing the community by staying alive? In any other field of increased government expenditure has there been a special minibudget? When Expo '67 was mooted, at a total cost of $180 million, did Mr. Sharp think to increase taxes by that exact amount so the public would know who was paying for what? When the Trans-Canada Highway was built, did Mr. Sharp deliver his prim Victorian lecture to the people?

We all know welfare costs money; we have been reminded of it often enough. But surely a program that allows a $75-a-month pensioner to go off a diet of porridge needs no public justification.

Stop! cries the business world. *You can't operate an economy in a vacuum. You want a guaranteed annual income for all, but how can we compete with the United States under such unequal conditions?*

The idea that we should do nothing until the Americans take the lead is deeply engrained in the Canadian consciousness. The fact is, however, that we do have a guaranteed annual wage for a large section of our population which the United States doesn't have. It is called the family allowance and it has not beggared us. A carefully planned and co-ordinated program of income maintenance does not reduce the total wealth of the nation – as, for instance, an expensive program of national defence does. Indeed, it can serve as a prime to the economic pump.

The evidence shows that there is one segment of the population that has more money than it can spend and another that has less than it needs. Obviously the guaranteed annual wage must be supported by people who have more than they can use. What is the point of amassing an enormous personal fortune when you can't take it with you?

Treason! You're saying a man shouldn't be able to save and provide for the future comfort of his children and grandchildren! That's the whole basis of our incentive system.

But should it be? Does an athlete pass on his long-distance track medals for his son to wear? Does the Nobel Prize also go to the grandchildren of the recipients? More to the point, if the country provides basic security – free education, medical care, and a guaranteed wage – to all as a right, what is the point of leaving large sums behind to grandchildren yet unborn?

But you're killing incentive! What will men work for if they aren't given the opportunity to accumulate a substantial share of this world's goods?

Yes: the New Democracy would kill incentive in misers. If a man's goal in life is purely and simply the hoarding of large sums of money, there'll be less incentive for him to do that. But it is my observation that, after a certain economic level is reached, the accumulation of money is not the chief incentive for most people. It never has been for those outside the business world, unless they are poor – the artists, teachers, writers, architects, yes, and to a large extent the doctors and engineers and others. (The very businessmen who keep talking about incentives are also quoted in the popular magazine profiles as saying they don't really care about the money; they work for the fun of it.) Money is certainly a status symbol; of that we are aware. As long as it is the criterion by which achievement is judged it will continue to be. But what is wrong with seeking better status symbols?

These arguments apply at the other end of the economic scale. Will a guaranteed annual wage kill incentive among the poor? If a man is given a certain amount of security, won't he quit working? Exactly the same contention could be made about the sons of the wealthy who are left large fortunes. Yet the evidence suggests that, given economic freedom, people will generally choose to do that which interests them most. It is up to society to see that these interests are widened and that too requires investment.

There is no point in repeating here what has already been said about foolish toil as opposed to creative leisure. At the present moment in history, the country is suffering a shocking loss as a result of the refusal of the well-to-do to invest in the underprivileged. When business leaders talk, as they do, about the waste in big government, they ought to consider the waste in human resources which the present system supports. The cost of poverty in terms of disease, disability, emotional breakdown, delinquency, and slums is staggering. We know that the highest proportion of our tubercular victims, the highest proportion of our emotionally distressed children and adults, the highest proportion of our juvenile delinquents, and the highest proportion of our criminals all come from the ranks of the impoverished. Sooner or later a statistically high proportion of these people become public charges. We pay to keep them in hospitals and jails where the costs are astronomical. It costs $3,000 a year to keep a man in jail, and this does not include the price of police or the courts, welfare costs for his family or community services for his dependants. In the words of Bessie Touzel, the former Executive Director of the Ontario Welfare Council: "Poverty is destroying people, increasing social health problems, and building a reckoning in ill health, social breakdown, and crime that is frightening to contemplate."

The highest proportion of physically ill people among us is to be found again in the ranks of the poor. Some are poor because they are sick but far more are sick because they are poor, because they cannot afford nutritious food, adequate housing, clothing, or preventive medical care. The Canadian Sickness survey showed that the poor, while sicker, receive less attention than other classes. The Carsons, mentioned by Maurice Sauvé, had never had dental attention. No one was surprised when the Family Service Association discovered that eleven of the twenty-five poor families it studied suffered from ill health. All were living on incomes below the bare minimum standards necessary for good health.

John Morgan, the social scientist, has said it:

It should be observed that Canadians already pay the cost of disease, social breakdown, inadequate housing, unemployment, and disability. The fundamental question is whether the cost should be paid by individual Canadians in the form of physical, social, or economic incapacity as well as accumulated debts, or whether, by an intelligent re-arrangement of the nation's affairs, those most able to do so will pay the costs of preventing avoidable distress and alleviating the human burdens now loaded on the backs of those least able to bear the load.

FOUR

Illusions about education

*Slavery is but half abolished, emancipation
is but half completed, while millions
of freemen with votes in their hands are left
without education. Justice to them,
the welfare of the States in which they live,
the safety of the whole Republic,
the dignity of the elective franchise,– all
alike demand that the still remaining
bonds of ignorance shall be unloosed and
broken, and the minds as well as
the bodies of the emancipated go free.*

ROBERT CHARLES WINTHROP'S
YORKTOWN ORATION (1881)

1. *Down with free education !*

Here and there, under flat stones and in dark crevices, one still encounters people who publicly and vociferously oppose the idea of free universal education in public schools. They are taken no more seriously today than those who supported the idea two centuries ago.

It is hard to believe that there was in my own grandfather's time a body of opinion as bitterly opposed to free education in grade schools as there has been in recent years opposed to free education in the universities or to a universal medical scheme. The arguments, more than a century ago, seem remarkably similar.

In the early Nineteenth Century, the idea that the sons and daughters of the working classes should receive anything more than a limited education was never successfully challenged. The prevailing establishment attitude was that the education of the upper classes demanded first priority; thus, aid to universities was considered before aid to highschools and aid to highschools before aid to elementary schools. In 1816, in Upper Canada, an act which would have given temporary support to "common schools" (as they were called) to the extent of $24,000 *per annum* was opposed by supporters of the Family Compact establishment. The reason? Because of a growing spirit of "insubordination and equality." Four years later the Family Compact succeeded in having the support reduced.

By mid-century the battle for free schooling was well-joined, thanks to the efforts of Egerton Ryerson. But it is important to recall that Ryerson's first bill in 1846, which would have established free public schooling of a sort based on a universal tax, was watered down by the legislature of Upper Canada. The rate bill was made assessable only upon the parents of children actually attending school. It was not until 1871 that the "common schools" actually became free in the wider sense and attendance compulsory, between the ages of seven and twelve, for four months of each year. But the idea that the education of the many is of benefit to *all* parents and to non-parents as well has had a hard time of it to this day.

The arguments against public education, by prominent public figures, politicians, ministers of the cloth, and newspapers as respectable and powerful as *The Globe* of Toronto, have a familiar ring to them when resurrected from the dust of old newspaper files. They have been used time and again, and are still being used, by members of the financial establishment in its war against new social measures. We have heard these same arguments employed during the twenty-year struggle for a national health scheme. And we hear them all again when a new form of free education is proposed: free university training for all who are able to benefit from it.

The old doctor-patient relationship argument, so dear to the hearts of the medical fraternity, comes through loud and clear in the words of the Hon. Robert Spence, Editor of *The Dundas Warder*, attacking the Common School Act in 1848:

The principle now disclosed is unjust, arbitrary, and inapplicable to the circumstances of Canada; more than this it is pregnant with the worst evils to the character and efficiency of our Public Seminaries of instruction. The tie which heretofore existed between the Teacher and the Parent of the taught is severed. Irresponsibility is the consequence and it becomes a matter of total indifference now how schools are conducted as long as the teacher's salary is provided.

Spence, a gifted writer who was to become a cabinet minister, was, we are told by J. C. Hodgins in his *Documentary History of Education in Upper Canada*, a man whose utterances can be "taken as a fair exponent of the current opinions of the day."

Another vocal opponent of free public-school education was the Rev. John Roaf who, in 1852, proposed a means test be applied to those accepting it:

We might give free education to those who otherwise would be destitute of it by making those purchase it who have the means . . . the free system divests the teacher of all proprietory and personal interest in the school . . . it will throw education into the hands of an electioneering party . . . it will render school attendance desultory and variable, because unpaid for, and always to be had for the asking.

The whole arsenal of tried-and-true weaponry was brought into play, especially between the years 1846 and 1852, to try to prevent tax money being spent to support public education. The blunderbuss of government waste and inefficiency was loaded and fired. Shafts labelled "means test" were loosed in volleys. Barrages of cannonballs bearing words like "freedom" and "state control" were laid down.

Communism was not the bugbear then that it has since become but it was actually dragged into the debate by the Rev. Mr. Roaf when he urged Upper Canadians to "spurn the unrighteous council which is introducing communism in education to the under-mining of property and society."

The Globe preferred the more familiar *bête noir* of "Prussian despotism," a favourite phrase in its editorials of that day: "Does Dr. Ryerson . . . countenance the doctrine that all children of the country should be under the guidance of the government of that country and ought to be educated at the will of the government whether the parents like it or not? Is this very scheme of gratis education not a part of Prussian despotism?"

As for "freedom," that overworked word was batted about like a shuttlecock. In 1848, the Standing Committee on Education in Toronto announced that the idea of taxing people who didn't have children in school was "repugnant to British Freedom and common sense." Letters to *The Globe* were peppered with references to rights and liberties: "There is extreme danger in the government extending its supposed sphere of usefulness in directions where it is sure to fly in the teeth of prejudice and rights and liberties of many of its subjects." All the polemics about the evils of state control, which have become familiar in the fight against the modern welfare state, were used more than a century ago. The Rev. Mr. Roaf, railing against free schooling, used the "extension of state control" argument: "Education is very desirable and all benevolent people should do what they can to secure it for every child . . . but as is a residence desirable, and firewood in the winter, and good clothes and medical aid when there comes sickness, but these being important does not show that the state should provide them."

The state was seen not only as an interloper but also as an inefficient and wasteful master. In 1847, *The Brockville Recorder* avowed that "more than one-third part of the government grant for education in Upper Canada is consumed or lavished in a manner which is useless, except for political purposes." At a public meeting called by the opponents of free schools in 1852, the chief antagonist, Angus Dallas, did his best to show that the free system was "inefficient and bad." At the same meeting one of the aldermen, speaking for his constituents, declared that "they would be satisfied if the schools were what they intended to be; but they found out in practice that they did not produce any benefit commensurate with cost."

The question of cost came up time and again, with the opposition insisting that most Canadians could afford to pay for the education of their children without the state introducing a system that dealt with rich and poor alike regardless of ability to pay. This view was summed up in *The Patriot* in 1848: "As a very large proportion of our population pay heavy sums for the education of their children at various schools with which this city abounds, it cannot be expected that they will quietly sit under this heavy taxation for the benefit of persons a large proportion of whom are fully as well able to pay the rates of the common schools as they."

"How few in this country cannot afford education?" asked a letter in *The Globe*. "People in general have a pretty keen sense of their own interest and in general are able and willing to pay for the education of their children. . . . I would be understood not to argue against the establishment of schools but against schools which are entirely gratuitous . . . against the principle of those who are able to pay but derive no benefit . . . this is the tyranny I denounce and describe as socialism."

Would it not be cheaper and more efficient, the antagonists argued, to provide free education for those who probably could not afford it rather than hand it out to everybody, rich and poor? The same arguments have been used in recent times by the opponents of family allowances for all, old age pensions for all, medical care for all, university education for all. These things are not seen as rights but as charities. Yet is anybody today prepared to go back to a school system where parents must take means tests or else pay fees?

Another argument in 1848, which is heard in our time, is that anything totally free wouldn't work because it wouldn't be valued. *The Globe*, dismissing the "pittance required for education" as unworthy of government subsidy, urged Ryerson to prove "that people who are so careless of their children's welfare as to be unwilling to take this trouble [to pay for schooling] will be in any way improved under a totally free system." *The Globe* opined that "experience has shown that that which costs nothing is valued at nothing; and we suspect that the unwillingness on the part of parents to send their children on a 'pauper' footing will be far from lessened under the new system."

The "state control saps initiative" argument, also familiar in our time, was trundled out. Thus a "Common School Taxpayer" writing to *The Globe* in 1852:

The pleas that more children would be sent to school if their fees were paid by direct taxation is utterly worthless. Will robbery on the part of the state elevate the masses? Does not past experience assure us that every act of injustice and wrong perpetrated by the stand tends to accelerate by tenfold ratio the downward tendency to degradation? Does not a man lose his self-respect when he reflects that to the purposes of his neighbours and not to the hard-earned gains of his fathers he owes whatever he possesses of education? . . . I hold that no state has a right, any more than an individual, to advance its interests by unjust means.

Stripped to essentials, the real argument against public education based on a universal property tax, was a simple one: "Why should people with no children in school have to help support the education of others?" Intrinsic to this view was the Puritan corollary that education is an individual and personal matter; and further, that it is of benefit only to those who receive it, that it has nothing to do with the spiritual or material wealth of the country as a whole. The idea that education in sum can be part of a new G.N.P., that it may indeed be essential to the future of the nation, is still not generally accepted. The same attitudes that stood in the way of free public-school education in Upper Canada in the 1840's have conspired against the democratization of education at higher levels in our own time.

---

2.   *Universities :*

Pastures for the privileged

We have been through the week and we have never listened to so much tripe. For twenty years we have tried to draw attention to the great successful men who left school at a very modest age. There was Ford, Edison, Lord Nuffield, Beaverbrook, St. Laurent, and Andrew Carnegie. . . . Ah, they say, those things don't happen now; you can't get ahead nowadays without plenty of education. That is complete rot. How do they know that?

> Jamieson Bone, President, Ontario
> Property Owners' Association,
> writing in *The Property Owner*,
> March, 1956

For the past century a series of myths has been fostered about education in Canada, and it seems clear that these myths have held back Canadian democracy and Canadian progress.

The major myths are these:

1. Anybody with the will to do so can get ahead in this country and rise to the top, no matter what his education, providing he works hard.

2. Our universities are truly democratic. To quote James Muir, President of the Royal Bank of Canada: "A university in Canada is not a class nursery, the paradise of the privileged, but the resort of young men and women of all classes and creeds who seek what it has to give."

3. Most students work their way through college.

4. Bright but needy students can usually get a bursary or a scholarship.

5. Those who don't attend college have only themselves to blame.

In 1965, a shattering book was published that banished these myths forever. It was Professor John Porter's study of social class and power in Canada, titled *The Vertical Mosaic*, perhaps the single most important Canadian work of the post-war years.

Briefly, Professor Porter showed that Canadian universities *are* pastures for the privileged, that upward mobility in our industrial society is largely a myth, that our attitudes toward education are apathetic, that there is a staggering amount of human waste in the land because so many Canadians are badly trained and educated, and that democracy, Canadian-style, is constricted, sterile, and a long way away from the universal ideal. This was not opinion on Professor Porter's part. It is documented fact not seriously questioned.

No one who reads *The Vertical Mosaic* can help but be outraged and scandalized by the short-sightedness of a WASP-dominated power elite so in-bred in its composition and so narrow in its attitudes that it has seriously stultified the spirit and potential of the nation. Porter's book runs to more than six hundred pages and only a portion of it – that dealing with university education – can be briefly summarized here; but it deserves to be read by every Canadian who cares about his country's future.

What Porter is able to demonstrate is that the country is run to a very large extent by people of inherited privilege who, if not snobs, certainly belong to a cosy in-group which resists encroachment from Jews, French Canadians, non-British immigrants, and upstarts from the lower classes. Twenty-two per cent of the economic élite – the most significant power bloc in the country – inherited their positions. More than one-third started out at or near the very top of the class system. A fantastic eighty-two per cent came from the middle class or above. And, significantly, those who rose from the lower classes were almost all born in a previous century. These may all be men of ability but it is clear that, in many cases, it wasn't mere ability that got them where they are today.

About one-third of the economic élite attended private schools. An examination of their origins shows that economic power in Canada belongs almost exclusively to the British even though this ethnic group made up less than half the population in 1951. Social mobility? It scarcely exists. Porter, in his examination of the top one hundred men in the economic élite – *la crème de la crème* – found that more than half had started out at or very near the top, and that only a small fraction, fifteen per cent, had been able to claw their way into the sacred preserve from below the middle class.

"The inequalities that exist in the social class system arise in part from the inadequacy of educational institutions," Porter says. "Thus as the corporate system becomes even more firmly established, the inequalities that arise because of parental position can be overcome only through a more open educational system."

Early in his book, Porter nails the "persistent myth that the drawback of an inadequate education can be overcome by experience in the work world." That may have been possible half a century ago, he says, but today "there seems to exist in the occupational world, not a ladder of continuous promotion, but rather hierarchical compartments into which people enter from the educational system." It's possible to move *within* a compartment but much more difficult to move from one compartment to another.

Equality of opportunity? Porter is able to demonstrate statistically, through D.B.S. figures, that higher education in Canada, much of it publicly subsidized, is a privilege of the upper classes.

ITEM: More than half the university students studied by D.B.S. in its 1956 investigation of their incomes and expenditures reported that their fathers were proprietors, managers, or professionals. Only 5.1 per cent of the students' fathers were classified as "labour," though this class makes up 20.5 per cent of the population.

ITEM: Children of the top four classes (out of eight) in Canada are heavily over-represented at university.

Class One children, with the highest paid fathers, are ten times over-represented. The lower three classes plus farmers (a separate group) are under-represented. *Half* the students attending university come from the top two classes.

ITEM: Education for the higher professions, such as law and medicine, is even more of a privilege of the upper income classes. In law and medicine the median family income of students' families was $6,293 and $5,663 respectively. (It is important here to distinguish between *median* and *average*. The median income is the income that lies exactly half way between the lowest income and the highest.)

ITEM: Almost one-quarter of the students surveyed by D.B.S. said that they had to postpone or water down their university training for lack of funds.

ITEM: Only five per cent of the undergraduate student income came from scholarships, prizes, and bursaries.

ITEM: Only one-third of student income came from summer jobs. The median expenditure for the educational year was $1,209; the median savings from a summer job was $507.

It is clear from a study of *The Vertical Mosaic* that the upper class in Canada is self-perpetuating, that in Porter's words "little has been done to remove barriers imposed by social conditions on the individual's educational opportunity," and that in this area Canada lags behind other Western industrial nations, particularly the United States.

What we are discussing here is human waste of the most appalling dimensions. All across Canada, tens of thousands of men and women are performing jobs which must seem deadly to them because they are equipped mentally to do so much better. How many potential brain surgeons (in a land short of doctors) are working at lathes? How many potential engineers are serving as file clerks? Men and women who ought to be planning the new

Canada – its cities, its social fabric, its political structure – are employed in menial and often silly tasks simply because economic conditions forced them to leave school too soon.

It is not enough to say, as some say, that they deserved what they got; by allowing such conditions the country deserves what it has got. In the words of Professor R. W. B. Jackson and Professor W. G. Fleming of the Ontario College of Education, "We seem to be doing an admirable job of squandering the priceless human resources available to us." These two researchers have estimated that the nation is utilizing to the full "the talents of probably no more than one-third of our academically gifted young men and women." Porter quotes the Paulend study of highschool students by Oswald Hall and Bruce McFarlane, who concluded that two-thirds of the students attending university could not be described as brilliant while only one-fifth of those who really *were* brilliant actually ever got there. And in Ontario, as a 1957 study by Professor W. G. Fleming shows, one-quarter of those who don't go to university have a better scholastic record than one-half who do. In Fleming's sample of 8,380 students, there were 1,423 who had a Grade XII average of more than seventy per cent who did not continue on to university. There were 3,281 who had an average *lower* than seventy. Of this group nearly half – 1,535 – were able to afford a university education. It's noteworthy that the students who *didn't* go almost equalled the numbers, with poorer marks, who did go. The same study makes it clear that sixty-six per cent of those highschool students uncertain about going to university would definitely go if they received a bursary.

To put it bluntly: If the country can afford to send only a certain number of students to university, then the wrong ones are generally being sent and this situation is having an adverse effect on all of us.

It is hard to escape the suspicion that Canadians have not put a very high premium on education, and certainly not as high a premium as Americans have. They have not pressed for educational reforms, they have not supported educational expenditures, and they have not invested to any great extent in the kind of training facilities needed to support a dynamic economy. But then why should we expect leadership here when the leaders come from the private schools and the moneyed classes? By and large we have not looked at our schools, technical colleges, and universities as an investment in the nation as valuable as an investment in a mine, a pulp mill, or an oil field. We have seen them rather as expensive nuisances, where "costs" are to be pared to the minimum and "frills" to be eliminated entirely. We cannot escape the Calvinist attitude to money – that it is something to be accumulated . . . that it is naughty to spend it.

The newspapers are sprinkled with tales about high educational costs (the term "investment" is never used) and municipal politicians constantly make headlines complaining about a rising millrate, which springs from the increasing price of education. In spite of the Canadian Sickness Survey's findings about the physical health of Canadians, gymnasiums and swimming pools have been considered wasteful and unnecessary. In spite of our cultural vacuum, school theatres have been anathema to municipal politicians so that budding actors and musicians have often had to make do with basketball courts. Every two-bit business in the country now has its own parking lot, but teachers still meet with resistance when they ask for space in which to park their cars. As for the state of their pay, it has long been a subject of bitterness and controversy.

This neanderthal municipal attitude was well summed up by Angus Campbell, President of the Ontario Association of Mayors and Reeves, when he spoke to their annual meeting in 1963:

Perhaps I am old-fashioned, but as a kid I went to the proverbial red schoolhouse, walked one mile and a half and was happy it was heated with a pot-bellied stove. Today we are ruining our children; not with education but with the frills of education. . . . We say to ourselves that we want our children's lives to be easier than ours. The result is that we are rearing a generation of monsters who feel and think that the world owes them a living. The world owes no one a living. Despite the fact that they did not ask to be born, the fact remains that they must carve their own future. . . .

What does the smug minority mean when it talks about "frills"? There are precious few real frills in the schools that I have seen. Are central heating, indoor washrooms, large windows, and comfortable desks and seats "frills"? Angus Campbell seems to think so, since these are what distinguish the new schools from the dark and airless brick buildings he eulogizes. What we have really been seeing is a grudging attitude to education as a whole – to new buildings, better teachers, and modern techniques. The same people who yearn for pot-bellied stoves will have no truck with audio-visual equipment. A school board faced with a public out-cry about parking space will think twice about ordering television sets, movie projectors, or record players for individual classrooms no matter how valuable these may be as educational tools.

In 1960, *The Property Owner* made its own position about education crystal clear in a blunt editorial which clearly suggested that too many schools were being built and too many teachers were being hired: "The university professor can lecture several hundred students at a time. Are collegiate students unable to learn some subjects in a similar manner? Who started this trend to small classes, anyway? . . . Some of the municipalities which protest about the burden of school costs have created or added to that burden by their own extravagances, by building schools which are too many and too fanciful."

When large businesses complain about high property taxes, they are really complaining about the cost of education, and when the business establishment opposes further "handouts" by govern-ment, it means, among other things, that it opposes free university or technical college education. It was surely no accident that, when the bogey of inflation was raised at Ottawa in the fall of 1966, the first casualty to Mitchell Sharp's axe was the government's promised $50 million university bursary project. It was obviously something the government felt it could postpone without undue public outcry; and it was right. No wonder Professor Porter talks about "the cultural factor of the relatively low evaluation of education." So rigid is higher education's position in the class structure that he finds "among the working classes, it is not yet seen as a choice at all; even when the economic situation permits it, the social situation mitigates against it."

Class in Canada, Porter has shown, determines the amount of education available. As a result the bottom third of Canadian society has little upward social mobility to look forward to. Porter thinks it would take at least a full generation of completely free higher education to change these attitudes; and he adds that a living allowance would perhaps be needed to accompany the free tuition before working-class youths of proven ability could take advantage of the opportunity. We have nothing like this yet and nothing like it in sight; indeed, we continue to postpone the smallest reforms, such as the federal bursary policy. If the business establishment has its way, the postponements are likely to continue, for whenever such reforms are suggested we hear the old shibboleths about freedom and liberty that were heard more than a century ago.

Listen, for example, to the President of Canadian Westinghouse, G. L. Wilcox, addressing the Canadian Manufacturers' Association:

In Russia, all educational institutions receive their support from the government. As a result, they must hew to the party's ideological tune. In technology, the Russians are evidently effective as witness the recent results of Russian science and engineering. But technology is one thing and freedom of thought and scholarship is another. Our technology must certainly be as good as Russia's . . . must be better if possible. But as far as freedom of thought, this is the very fabric of our Western philosophy. Our institutions of learning must be free . . . they ought to obtain support from a variety of sources if this freedom is to be guarded. They must not be dependent on any one source for money. Only under these circumstances will they be able to resist all efforts on the part of anyone, to limit freedom to learn, to think, or to explore, to investigate, to expound.

This attitude can be seen to be an extension of the same ideology that opposed free common schools in 1848. What has been its legacy? Again Professor Porter has outlined the problem. Lacking educational facilities of our own, we have sought to import people already trained in other countries, thus postponing again the desperate need for educational reform in Canada.

ITEM: In 1962, thirty-five per cent of all the doctors registering to practice in Canada were graduates of foreign medical schools.

ITEM: For most of the years of the 1950's, between five and

six thousand Canadians were forced to take their advanced training in the United States.

ITEM: About thirty-five per cent of all those interviewed by the federal Department of Labour for a 1956 study of five skilled occupations in Canada received the greater part of their training outside the country.

ITEM: During the 1950's, about two-fifths of the estimated new professional jobs and an estimated one-half of the new skilled jobs were filled by immigrants.

Faced with this indisputable evidence, can anyone say smugly (as some do say smugly) that our educational system is up to date? Can anyone pretend that a penny-pinching and selfish attitude to educational investment has been anything but disabling? Can anyone continue to believe the clichés about freedom and liberty resting foursquare on a system of university privilege? Surely future generations will see this one as we see the die-hards of 1848, selfish, narrow, short-sighted men, unable to grasp the vision of the future, imprisoned by a bookkeeping attitude to life, creeping silently and blindly along at the tag end of the parade of progress.

---

3. *An under-investment*
    in human beings

Although it is obvious that people acquire useful skills and knowledge, it is not obvious that these skills and knowledge are a form of capital, that this capital is in substantial part a product of deliberate investment, that it has grown in Western societies at a much faster rate than conventional (non-human) capital, and that its growth may well be the most distinctive feature of the economic system. It has been widely observed that increases in national output have been large compared with the increases of land, man-hours, and physical reproducible capital. Investment in human capital is probably the major explanation for this difference.

Much of what we call consumption constitutes investment in human capital. Direct expenditures on education, health, and internal migration to take advantage of better job opportunities are clear examples. Earnings foregone by mature students attending school and by workers acquiring on-the-job training are equally clear examples. Yet nowhere do these enter into our national accounts. The use of leisure time to improve skills and knowledge is widespread and it, too, is unrecorded. In these and similar ways, the QUALITY *of human effort can be greatly improved and its productivity enhanced. I shall contend that such investment in human capital accounts for most of the impressive rise in the real earnings per worker.*

> Theodore W. Schultz,
> *The American Economic Review*,
> March, 1961

Business spokesmen are fond of pointing out that Canada has one of the highest per capita income rates in the world. As we have seen, they often couple this boast with a plea for a continuation of a *laissez-faire* economic system in which every man will be allowed to fend for himself without the help of the state. The high income level and the free enterprise system, they intimate, go hand in hand. Allow government handouts with resultant tax increases, and the income level will drop. This argument has been used to shore up attacks on everything from increased welfare payments to bigger subsidies for universities.

What these speakers fail to say is that the per capita income in Canada has remained consistently about one-quarter below that of the United States since the turn of the century. It is now clear that a substantial portion of this income gap is tied directly to the fact that the United States has a more democratic educational system than our own. Traditionally, state universities in the United States have enjoyed a comparatively low fee structure; in some states, in fact, university education has been entirely free, as far as tuition is concerned.

The evidence is to be found in another remarkable book, Gordon W. Bertram's study for the Economic Council of Canada, *The Contribution of Education to Economic Growth*, published in June of 1966. For anybody who cares about the future of Canada, Professor Bertram's disclosures are as disturbing as Porter's. He makes it clear that this would be a wealthier country with a higher standard of living if our educational investment had been greater and our policy more farsighted.

Bertram points out that in the early years Canada's record in education was a good one. The country made spectacular gains in the latter part of the Nineteenth Century right up until World War I. Literacy and elementary education for all citizens were vigorously promoted. But then "it appears as though the democratic spirit which had promoted universal elementary education in Canada failed to operate to the same extent in secondary education efforts and education beyond elementary school continued to be the prerogative of the élite." (Highschool fees in most parts of Canada weren't abolished until the Twenties or later.)

Until 1911, Bertram's statistics show, the educational attainments of the Canadian and American labour forces were fairly close. But after this date the gap began to widen, and after 1920 the United States pulled ahead of Canada at an alarming rate. The gap widened decade by decade so that by the 1960's the absolute gap between the American and Canadian labour forces in terms of median years of schooling had reached two years.

At every level of schooling, American attainments for all age groups are above Canadian. What is most disturbing is that, among the younger members of the labour forces of the two countries, the gap is widest. For example, only 28.2 per cent of Canadian male workers between the ages of twenty-five and thirty-four have had four years of highschool. The figure for American males is 57.2 per cent! The gap in university education is even more disturbing. Only six per cent in Canada have university degrees; the figure in the United States is 14.7 per cent.

Similarly the highschool dropout rate in Canada is far higher than it is south of the border. Figures on rising retention rates from Grade IX through Grade XI suggest that Canada is thirty years behind the United States.

Bertram says that, even though the trend appears to have started to reverse, "it would nevertheless require years to narrow the gap . . . to any significant degree." And he adds: "An acceleration of this process would be possible only through strong and sustained efforts to raise the average education of young people in Canada to even higher levels and to introduce measures to raise the educational level of the existing labour force."

Is the country prepared to make such a massive investment? The minimum that is required is better schools, higher paid teachers, better and more modern teaching equipment which takes the electronic revolution into account, free education right through university and beyond, and, probably, a system of subsidies which would in effect pay the best students a salary on an increasing scale to pursue their studies to the end point. Given the current attitude to "frills" and "handouts," one can hold only a dim hope for such a revolution. The nation which has subsidized a transcontinental railway, a St. Lawrence waterway, and a world exposition is unlikely to put up a fraction of those investments for a modern and democratic educational system. Such things can be seen; but education is ephemeral.

In the world of the future, when the problem of leisure becomes pressing, the need for an educated citizenry will be equally pressing. Yet right now there is substantial evidence that, apart from the benefits of the spirit, education pays off in dollars and cents. Consider these comparisons between the United States and Canada, culled from Professor Bertram's statistical findings.

ITEM: Between 1911 and 1961, income per man – considering only the years of schooling – increased almost twice as much in the United States as it did in Canada.

ITEM: Over the past thirty years the contribution of education to increasing the productivity of the United States labour force was almost double the Canadian record.

ITEM: Canadian average income would be from seven to eight per cent higher, other things being equal, if the

Canadian labour force had attained the educational
levels prevailing in the United States.

The idea that education can be treated as an investment and
that a specific rate of return can be measured from an educational
program is a new and intriguing concept; but some fascinating
calculations have been made on precisely this point. Theodore
Schultz, quoted at the head of this chapter, has pioneered in this
field. He estimates that if education were treated purely as an
investment its returns would be seen as "relatively more attractive
than those to non-human capital." Bertram has investigated the
various other studies made in the United States on the subject.
When *all* costs of education are totted up: university students'
private expenses, earnings foregone by extra time spent in college,
other university costs borne by the government (including even
those taxes that might be levelled on campus property if colleges
were not exempt), the social rate of a return on a university
education is estimated at between eight and eleven per cent *per
annum*, falling well within the rate of return on business capital.
Private returns to the individual (apart from the general return to
society) are somewhat higher, exceeding twelve per cent *per annum*
in the case of university education. This, of course, leaves aside
the obvious non-material benefits that come with a better educated
populace, involving a whole spectrum of values and aspirations.

It is ironical that, in the face of this body of evidence, newspaper editorials and business leaders continue to insist that
productivity can best be increased if Canadians work harder. It
would be more realistic to call for greater educational expenditures. Between 1911 and 1961, in Canada, twenty-five per cent of
the rise in productivity per employed person was accounted for
by educational improvements. What might that increase not have
been had we taken a more progressive attitude to schools and
colleges!

What we have seen in Canada, over the past half century, is
what Schultz has called "an under-investment in human beings."
We have cheerfully poured money into everything but people. We
have had land booms and railway booms, mining booms and
building booms. But we have been scandalously wasteful with our

human resources. Our inability to cope with or invest in human welfare, health, and education has not saved us tax money; it has cost us all dearly. And we will be paying for this neglect for generations to come.

---

4. *The poor can't go to college*

The country is in deep trouble educationally and the assault on ignorance will have to be a massive one on many fronts. Free university education of itself will not solve our dilemma; that much is obvious. It is not merely lack of money that conspires against the lower classes; it is the total social environment. The subconscious Canadian attitude – that higher education is the preserve of the élite – needs to be changed.

Thanks to the Canadian Welfare Council's detailed study of the urban poor in 1965, we now have some insights into the attitudes of the poor to higher education. These were effectively summed up by Lillian Thomson in her case report on fifty families living in poverty in Saint John, N.B. The school system in Saint John is a reasonably strong one; with a possible exception, the "ghetto school" does not exist. The normal child therefore has the means of a good education, seemingly within his grasp. What happens? Here is Miss Thomson's summary:

* He measures himself by the modest attainments of family and neighbourhood, with their lack of mental stimulation and possibly their incomprehension of intellectual interests.

* He is living where the immediate concrete problems are so compelling that there is little family influence toward establishing the long-range view, to put off the immediate if short-lived status and security of an unskilled job.

* He goes to school hungry or half-hungry.

* He goes to school tired, from flats in which children do not get their rest through noise or cold or crowding.

* He loses time by being sent home with lice or impetigo. He is re-infected and there are many short drop-outs before the final drop-out.

A similar situation exists in adult retraining schemes. Saint John has facilities with good standards but only two or three men have managed to take advantage of these, Miss Thomson reports. "The others believed that their access to these facilities was blocked by their rudimentary basic education, by the cost of the courses, and by the impossibility of supporting their families during lengthy training programs."

At the other end of the nation, in Vancouver, where the educational attainments of the poor tend to be higher, similar conclusions were reached: "The problem is not so much the difficulty of physical access nor the lack of educational facilities. . . . It is rather the failure, for many complex reasons, of both adult and adolescent either to perceive the need for additional educational or vocational skills or to find ways of using the opportunities open to acquire them."

Here are the significant items from R. A. Jenness' study of fifty poor families in Vancouver:

* "There is no doubt that the poor are very conscious of their educational inadequacies, and hope for better things for their children. It is not clear how far their expectations are fulfilled – the evidence in our survey suggests that although the children go somewhat further than their parents only a few take full advantage of the educational possibilities open to them."

* "Few adults evinced much immediate interest in taking re-training courses. 'It was impossible with the children' . . . 'I couldn't afford it now.' Many spoke vaguely of taking re-training sometime – but probably never will unless they are forced by bitter circumstances or encouraged by more positive inducements than exist today."

✳ "It is virtually impossible for a married man with children to secure general highschool training during the day over any meaningful period without going heavily into debt. Here again the poor appear to be disadvantaged compared to other social groups. The federal government provides interest-free loans and a generous system of scholarships and bursaries to university students whose future income levels will probably far exceed those in the poverty category. But no such liberal sources of financial capital are available to persons in the least skilled levels who probably need the additional education most of all."

Dozens of detailed case reports from four major Canadian cities flesh in these skeletal statements. The names are fictitious but the circumstances are real:

THE FISHERS OF VANCOUVER: A fifty-seven-year-old fish grader in poor health, Mr. Fisher has two of his seven children living with him, a son twenty, and a daughter nineteen. Both are highschool drop-outs. The whole family is in poor health and the son is unemployed and on welfare. The daughter felt she was discriminated against in her highschool because of her poor background. There is a general defeatist attitude to education on the part of both children.

THE LANGLEYS OF SAINT JOHN: They and their five children, aged from fourteen years to six weeks, live in three rented rooms. The family is heavily in debt for medical expenses, furniture, etc. There is no place for the children to play except in the streets. The oldest boy works every night after school in a drug store in order to help his mother. Sometimes he is almost too tired to get up for school. Though he seems to have ability, he failed the previous year.

THE JOHNSONS OF TORONTO: Mr. Johnson, who is illiterate, is employed irregularly. Both he and his wife are in ill health. His twelve-year-old son wants to be a doctor but this seems out of the question since the family can't even afford dental care for their two boys. The Johnson's main hope is that their boys will finish highschool.

THE CHARLEBOIS OF MONTREAL: This family of eight are crammed into six rooms above a store. The fifty-eight-year-old father makes about $38 a week as a helper in furniture repair. The mother suffers from ulcers and nervous tension. Two of the children are tubercular. The eldest boy, now twenty-two, had to leave school after Grade VI. He's a doorman at a cinema and makes a small salary. The father hopes the others will finish highschool.

THE GREGORYS OF VANCOUVER: This fatherless family of eight children lives "in the worst housing conditions of all the families interviewed." The front steps are so badly broken the postman refuses to deliver the mail. Mrs. Gregory's existence is nomadic since landlord after landlord objects to eight children. The mother, not surprisingly, is being treated for ulcers and a nerve condition. Four of her children are slow learners and have failed grades, but Mrs. Gregory hopes that her two sons, aged fourteen and ten, who have the intellectual capacity, will complete highschool and perhaps go on to university. Says the case worker: "She is unable to recognize that the present home environment is not conducive for a child to concentrate and study."

THE EMERYS OF SAINT JOHN: This family of six lives on Mr. Emery's monthly $253 (as a labourer) in a dilapidated, rat-infested house in the slum area, described as "unfit for habitation." It is so cold in winter that the two small, dark bedrooms must be closed off and the children packed into the livingroom. The ceilings are falling in, the wiring is make-shift, and there is no hot water. The family desperately wants a larger place with privacy for the two older girls, aged fifteen and twelve, where they could be "quiet to study." Both parents seek an education for their children. The girls want to be nurses. But they all foresee difficulty in keeping up a standard of clothing and expense money at the highschool level.

THE DUPUIS OF MONTREAL: Two adults and seven children live in a four-room house described as "pitiable." The mother's idea of heaven is a home where the boys and the girls could have two rooms between them – one for each sex. At present all live and sleep in a single bedroom. Conditions are filthy and chaotic. One daughter left school at Grade IX and now, at the age of fourteen, contributes to the family income by working in a box factory. Mr. Dupuis hopes his sons will go as far as Grade XI but feels eight years of school is plenty for girls "to wash diapers." He would not support a lengthy term of education for his boys.

It's significant that not one of the parents in these case histories had any more than a Grade VIII education. Several had much less. Yet most hoped for something better for their children. The insistent press campaign against drop-outs has convinced large numbers of people that their children ought to be educated; but it has not shown them *how* they can get that education. In Toronto, the Welfare Council discovered that ninety-four per cent of the poor families interviewed wanted their children to go to college; yet only fourteen per cent were able even to partially finance a higher education: "The optimism of these parents is remarkable in that they will be unable to help their children achieve the expected educational attainment." The findings were similar in the other test cities.

In his report on urban poverty in Toronto, Dr. Wilson Head echoes Professor Porter and Professor Bertram in calling for a massive economic program to raise the educational standards of the nation. He urges economic and educational "aids" for all children in low-income neighbourhoods as well as programs "designed to help the child overcome the handicaps of poor educational and socio-economic background."

Translated, this is a blunt appeal for subsidies. In short, we are going to have to pay bright scholars to continue on at high-school and at college. The choice is really a simple one: we can pay them now and get value for our money; or we can pay them later, when they go on relief, and in effect toss our money out into the streets.

We can, of course, predict the reaction that a plan of such boldness would receive from the smug minority. Indeed, we can write a speech for the new c.m.a. president to use at the next annual meeting:

"Far be it from me, gentlemen, to want to put the clock back. That is not my purpose today. All of us, I believe, want the very best for our fellow men; and I yield to no one in my desire to see this country continue strong through a sane and realistic educational policy. But surely the time has finally come when we must cry, 'Halt!' to any further handouts. It is all very fine to say that we would like to have certain gifts from an all-powerful state. But who is to pay for these gifts? Where is the money coming from? You don't get something for nothing, gentlemen; we all pay for these hidden educational frills through our hard-earned tax dollars. What the government hands out from one pocket, it takes back from us into another. Now it is my conviction that we have in this free nation an educational system second to none in the world! And I want to see that system keep pace! But to suggest that every Tom, Dick, and Harry who isn't prepared to pull himself up by his bootstraps at highschool should be coddled by the state with free goodies is to fly in the face of economic reality. This, I submit to you, weakens the very moral fibre of the nation. Surely, gentlemen, a proper education depends on a little perspiration! Does it really hurt to struggle a little? Do we not learn through struggle to appreciate the bounties of this land? Was it not struggle that made this country what it is today? Let us never forget one thing, gentlemen. When an all-powerful state removes incentive . . . then freedom itself – the freedom that you and I and our pioneering forefathers struggled for – that freedom, I say, is in peril!" (*Prolonged and sustained applause*)

5. *Why can't learning
be fun?*

In the age of the computer, when the mass of the people are freed from toil and want, education will assume an importance totally unrecognized today. For without education in an age of leisure there can be no freedom.

One cannot begin to guess what forms education will take in the future; one can only predict with certainty that they will be varied and that the formalized school system, if it exists at all, will provide only one of many paths down which the learner will stroll.

It is one thesis of this book that, apart from future considerations, the country must now be prepared to accept a totally free educational system. Such a system would involve much more than free schooling at university and post-graduate levels for bright students. It would involve the paying of salaries to those who continued their studies, and it would involve raising the salaries of those who showed themselves able to go on and on. (We do this now, of course, to a limited extent with certain professors who rarely make an appearance in a teaching classroom but remain at university for study and research.) Thus, some men and women would be students all their lives and the state would subsidize their studies.

More than that, the time is swiftly arriving when it may be necessary for large numbers of people to go back to school again to pick up knowledge that did not exist when they graduated. It is not too much to expect that a second four- or five-year university course and perhaps an entirely new career await large numbers of people after the age of forty. When this necessity arises we should not shrink from footing the bill any more than we shrink from refurbishing a power plant when it becomes obsolete or rebuilding a railway when the ties rot.

But a modern educational system, geared to such an expansion, must take into account the new techniques of communication.

There is very little evidence that this has been seriously or vigorously considered in Canada.

Surely the saddest spectacle of Canada's Centennial Year was that of the minister of education of the country's richest province pleading with a government board to set aside just one channel in the city of Toronto for educational television.

Torontonians are bombarded by commercial television. They get three local channels and three more from the United States, all of them carrying commercial programs of varying merit. Surely in any country that cares a fig for education the seventh channel would, after nearly twenty years of the hard sell, be reserved for something else. It is a measure of our national attitudes that nobody seemed to take William Davis's proposal very seriously.

Shortly afterwards, Toronto learned that it was going to have a seventh commercial television station beamed at it! There was a public outcry, but the outcry had nothing whatsoever to do with the lack of one educational outlet. The public was distressed over the possibility that the new station might get in the way of American commercial programming from Buffalo.

At the end of 1967, there was still not a single educational television station in Canada operating on the UHF band (to which most sets are exclusively tuned). The decision on the seventh Toronto channel had been postponed, but few seriously believed that it would eventually be reserved for the Ontario Department of Education. The business world long ago recognized that television was the most potent educational medium available and it has made good use of it. So far the medium has been denied the schools, and there has been no public outcry over this scandal. One must conclude that people get the kind of education they deserve.

Nobody can expect the politicians to give any sort of a lead here since the politicians, least of all, understand the new medium. When they use it at all, which is rarely, they use it atrociously, and they have made a law which prevents them, specifically, from using it dramatically.

It is a measure of our political perception that most candidates for office continue to use the Nineteenth Century medium of the public meeting during election campaigns. In this they are supported by the press. One would think Sir John A. Macdonald were still running for office.

Consider this situation:

John Foster Blodgett, M.P., is standing once again for office in the constituency of Landmark South. Following time-honoured tradition, his campaign manager hires a series of halls and arranges a series of public meetings through various organizations, which J. F. Blodgett will address.

J. F. Blodgett prepares a speech for each of these meetings. It is actually the same speech with various new openings and some of the paragraphs shuffled about. At his campaign manager's suggestion Blodgett has extra copies of his speech made for the press, so that they will not actually have to go to the meetings that Blodgett addresses.

At this point Blodgett rebels. He hates addressing meetings. Most of the time only the front rows are filled and he knows all the people there are going to vote for him anyway. Why give the same speech night after night to a handful of the converted?

"Look," says Blodgett, "let's save time and money. Feed the speeches to the press and cancel the meetings."

"If you cancel the meetings the press won't publish the speeches," his campaign manager points out

"But they don't even *go* to the meetings!" poor Blodgett expostulates.

"Doesn't matter," says his campaign manager. "If you don't actually read these speeches then it isn't news."

Then Blodgett has a brilliant idea. Why not, he suggests, give one speech on television? That way he'll reach far more people. But his campaign manager sadly reminds him that the press doesn't generally consider a speech made on television to be news. He'll have a better chance of making headlines if he speaks to half a dozen of his friends in a public hall.

So Blodgett delivers a speech that the press has already read, and doesn't bother to hear, to a small group of his supporters and next day, on the page that handles the election coverage, he reads, to his satisfaction that BLODGETT FLAYS INCREASED TAXES, PLEDGES NEW ECONOMIES.

Meanwhile my three-year-old child is sitting at home watching

Steve Reeves in *Hercules* and unwittingly (and unbeknownst apparently to the politicians, the press, and the educators) getting a wild, free-wheeling, utterly unco-ordinated education that is far more potent than anything the schools can offer at present. By the time she reaches kindergarten, two years hence, she will be infinitely more sophisticated than any kindergarten child of the 1920's or even the 1940's.

Television, soaking through her pores, will have taken her outside the narrow confines of home and community and conditioned her to accept a world of infinite variety, full of people of odd shapes and colours who act and speak in a different way. Parochialism for such a child is no more than a word.

As well, television will have taught her a good deal about history, geography, and the arts. She will be familiar with the myths of Hercules and Ulysses from the old movies; she will know something about King John of England and the longbow from the Robin Hood series; she will have seen what Hong Kong, black Africa, and New York look like on "Walt Disney," "I Spy," and "The Man from Uncle." She will even have been exposed to bits of modern dance, opera, and symphony music. (She will also have soaked up a set of truly appalling values.) Most of this she will have accepted subliminally, and a great deal of what she accepts will be distorted, but it will be there nonetheless.

Finally, television will condition her to receive knowledge in a different fashion from her parents: by means of a swiftly moving series of images, many of them totally unrelated and arranged in an illogical manner. She will, for example, be exposed to an image of a half-naked man swinging on a jungle vine, to be followed instantly and without explanation by another image of a beagle munching something from a bowl on a modern kitchen floor, to a third image of a man in a pith helmet with a rifle in his hand. She will not be bewildered by this. She will accept the fact that the dog is appearing in a pet food commercial and is a separate story from the "Tarzan" series. But that same sequence of images, thrown on a screen, would baffle and confuse a Boer War general.

What happens to this sophisticated and conditioned youngster when she finally arrives at school? She will sit in a circle, just as her parents did when they were the same age; she will colour pictures: she will sing songs; she will be read to from books. Will she be shown anything on television? It is not likely. Nor will it be likely in the grades that follow.

For the remainder of her days in school – or so it appears at this juncture – people will read to her from books or lecture to her from notes, and she will copy down what they say and say it back to them. That is the way things stand at public school, highschool, and university twenty years after television was captured by the commercial media.

Can we blame this child if, after several years of scribbling in a ruled exercise book notes dictated to her from a platform, she drops out of school from sheer boredom? There was a time when the school was the only source of information and the only medium of education, but that time is long past and if the schools are to compete with the advertising agencies they must accept the new electronic world and – perhaps more difficult still – the public must accept it too.

The public still considers a TV set to be a luxury, in spite of the fact that almost every family now within range of a channel has one. When welfare cases or people in public-housing develop-ments are discovered to own television sets, there is invariably an outcry, as there was in the Regent's Park development in Toronto in its early years. Yet television, not religion, has become the opiate of the people today and especially of the poor. Time and again, the Social Welfare Council's studies of poor families in urban and rural areas revealed that the *only* entertainment was provided by the TV set. One shudders to think what life would be like for large numbers of people – the aged, the sick, and the underprivileged who cannot afford a theatre, concert, or movie ticket – were it not for the nightly glow that the home set casts over the parlour. For these people TV is the only form of adult education they are likely to get. This makes television the single most powerful educational medium in the country. Yet it is not used as such.

The attitude of many university professors to television as a teaching medium is snobbish, unconcerned, and uninformed. Some of them take the Puritan attitude that education shouldn't be fun. They talk about "academic disciplines" in the same way the Calvinists talked about work disciplines. It doesn't occur to them apparently that the disciplines can continue no matter what the teaching medium.

Others simply don't understand the medium itself. I was flabbergasted while working on this book to discover that a good many academics apparently think they are using television to its fullest by televizing existing lectures. They cannot get it into their heads that the techniques of an old medium are not the techniques of the new. It is as if one filmed a three-act play and called it a movie.

No one is suggesting that the personal touch be dispensed with in the universities. We must still have a relationship between professor and student (though that relationship is worn precious thin in some of the larger lecture halls on the major campuses).

Seminars are fundamental to higher learning; my own complaint at university was that there weren't enough of them. But as long as television exists, no man should ever again have to read a set of notes to a class of scribblers. And, if we are to have universal university education for the new age of leisure than we *must* start to use the electronic media.

Is it more effective to read *Hamlet* to the class or see it performed on the screen?

Is it more effective to talk about the resources of Brazil from a textbook or to see a documentary on that country?

Is it more effective to show molecular structure by a series of textbook drawings or to have those drawings animated on a moving screen in colour?

This sort of thing is being attempted on a limited scale in one or two campuses in Canada. (Scarborough College, Toronto, is an effective example.) But many academics are repelled by any departure from traditional teaching.

Many others, who accept the principle, balk at the price. "What university can afford to produce documentaries, plays, animated cartoons?" they ask. The answer is that no single university can or no single highschool or elementary school; but to think now of these as closed units, islands unto themselves, is madness. The universities as a group are perfectly well-equipped to parcel out the work and then to exchange it in the same way that large business corporations parcel out the entertainment and combine, through network facilities and electronic tape, to present sixteen hours of television every day of every week. The business world solved its educational (or propaganda) problems twenty years ago. It tells us something about our time and our system of values that the educational world is more than a generation behind.

---

6   *Dialogue with myself*

SELF: This whole book is full of inconsistencies.

ME: What? Where? Show me one.

SELF: In the first part of the book you attack the present educational system as totalitarian. You say it's causing students to drop out of highschool. Now you say that if we have *more* of it for more people, the country will be better off.

ME: Not more of the same. More of something better. But even if we had more of the same it would be better than less.

SELF: Oh? Are you really arguing that a bad education is better than –

ME: Than *no* education? Yes. I don't believe that television at present gives five-year-olds an ideal education. But it's still an improvement on nothing.

SELF: Pat Watson has said this about the "education" that commercial television gives: "Situation comedies, I-Spies, animated cartoon series, and the Ed Sullivan show reflect subtly and powerfully the main ethical and cultural orientations of our Western society. Many of these themes are pretty appalling. They reiterate with quiet conviction our basic, unquestioned myths of progress and the quest for power and happiness.

They tell us over and over again that a new object is better than an old object, that an object is better than a person, that persons are individuals of less importance than a group. They say that controversy and individual thought are dangerous and should be eschewed. They say that 'Citizenship' is more value than Personhood. They show tomorrow as inevitably better than today, which is a pernicious lie, and one of the most destructive myths of our society. And they urge the seeking of safety and the avoidance of adventure." Would you agree with that?

ME: Yes, I think I would, in essence –

SELF: And you still say it's better than nothing?

ME: If that's all that television did for children I would agree. But it's only part of what they get. As I've written earlier it also gives children – and adults – a window on the world. This is the good side of bad television. Children do arrive at school with an utterly different outlook than they once did and that has to be taken into consideration.

SELF: Do you really believe that educational television is the key to the schools and colleges of the future?

ME: No. It's only one of several keys just as schools and colleges will only be one of several forms of education in the future. But we cannot dismiss the fact of television as a teaching tool. It's there whether we like it or not. Children are being subjected now to an intensive educational process long before they learn to read. Moreover they are being *conditioned* to this particular process. Why not make use of this conditioning?

SELF: But isn't this being done already?

ME: What's being done is a drop in the bucket to what could be done. Educational television is still in the gimmick stage. But let me make it clear that I am using the attitude toward television here simply as a symbol of a broader attitude to education. I just don't think the country is keeping up with the times. The attitude to TV in the schools is on a par with the attitude to long hair in the schools. We are still thinking in Nineteenth Century terms.

SELF: But aren't *you* also thinking in Nineteenth Century terms?

ME: How's that?

SELF: You argue earlier in this book that the day is coming when toil will be obsolete . . . when the "job," as we know it, will be obsolete. But you seem to be equating university education with jobs. You talk of productivity tied to educational attainment, and you show university education in terms of a percentage return on investment.

ME: Certainly. First, because here we've been examining the past half-century and not the future; and second, because it's necessary to convince people that universal education is an investment and not an expense.

SELF: You're avoiding the point. If, as you say, the day is coming when two per cent of the people provide everything the rest need, then of what value is your argument about education as an investment?

ME: Of even greater value than it is now. Surely education must be the chief investment of a leisure society. In a really free society – that is a society in which both toil and want have been reduced to minimums – then everybody *must* be educated to the limits of his abilities.

SELF: Are you suggesting it be compulsory, then? Is that your idea of a free society?

ME: Certainly not. I would hope the options would be so attractive that all would seek to exercise them. But first we must change attitudes. If we maintain our Nineteenth Century outlook – that education is an expense rather than an investment, that it cannot be universal because we can't afford it, that so-called "frills" are luxuries our collective pocket books can't stand – then we enter the age of leisure under the same handicaps that have dogged us for the past fifty years: we simply waste the human potential of more than half the population.

SELF: Are you advocating unlimited spending then on the educational system of the future?

ME: Not really. What I am advocating is that we treat education in exactly the same way that we treat highways. Let me sum up the attitude: Every time a man drives an automobile over a hole in the pavement he says, "Why the hell don't they widen these roads?" But when new school goes up he hollers about expense. I'd like the day to come when men and women walk into new schools, look over the equipment, size up the teachers, check the curriculum, and say: "It's nice but it still isn't good enough. Can't we make it a little better?" When we talk and think in those terms then we can, in good conscience, boast freely about our progress.

THE PARADE OF PROGRESS

The march of social progress is like a long and straggling parade, with the seers and prophets at its head and a smug minority bringing up the rear.

The parade is seen to be led by clowns, beating on battered cymbals and carrying placards bearing strange and frightening inscriptions: ABOLISH CAPITAL PUNISHMENT FOR CHILDREN. . . . FREE EDUCATION UP TO GRADE VIII. . . . SUNDAY STREETCARS. . . . RELIEF FOR THE UNEMPLOYED. . . . PUBLICLY OWNED HYDRO POWER. . . . LEGALIZED BIRTH CONTROL. . . . GRADUATED INCOME TAX. . . . SPORTS ON SUNDAY. . . . WIDER DIVORCE LAWS. . . . BILL OF RIGHTS. . . . GUARANTEED ANNUAL WAGE. There was a time when the placards all read: LOVE THY NEIGHBOUR. In our time they read MAKE LOVE NOT WAR.

If the parade is headed up by clowns it is because the spectators see them as clowns, oddly garbed and unconventionally shorn. They are called dreamers, sometimes, or wild-eyed idealists or dangerous radicals or fuzzy-minded do-gooders or simply goofs and nuts. The nuts pass by in nondescript order, getting a laugh here and a cat-call there, banging discordantly on battered brass, waggling their beards and waving their banners . . . and then there is a gap in the parade.

The next group in the parade is composed largely of artists and poets with here and there a novelist and the occasional radical essayist and the odd – the *oh*-so-odd – religious heretic. They have caught the echo of the nuts and the goofballs far up ahead, and they are busily repeating it after their several fashions and even translating it, somewhat obscurely, for the multitudes. The police watch them carefully, keeping them in line when they step out of the parade. The crowd obviously enjoys them but does not take them seriously. Though they are listened to, it is generally their form, not their content, that appeals. They are said to be ahead of themselves in the parade; and besides they do not wear business suits.

The group that follows along behind them does not all wear business suits either, though some have taken on this protective camouflage. But most of them have shirts with cuffs and ties of a sort; and the occasional sports jacket now makes its appearance. In this group are the young radical labour leaders just up from the rank-and-file and full of unworkable ideas with which to challenge the establishment. They march shoulder-to-shoulder with the perennially unsuccessful independent candidates for public office – frustrated aldermen, long-time mayorality contenders, deposit-losers of various stripes, clinging stubbornly to their impossible theories in the face of massive public indifference. Right behind them, in a kind of chirping cluster, we find the way-out teachers and assistant professors, all of them subject to the kind of amused indulgence that passes for academic freedom.

There is another gap in the parade. Then, round the corner, we catch the bright plumage of fluttering banners and we hear the noise of drums. The spectators cheer the drummers, for they are a popular crowd of rowdies. There are priests here – radical but not heretical – and they are well-known to the populace, for their mildly alarming views have titillated thousands of newspaper readers. Mingling with them, shoving and pushing, blowing on tin whistles and hammering endlessly on the drums, are the popular radio and newspaper commentators, the outspoken hosts of open-line radio shows, the crusading columnists, the perennial TV panelists, the sociologists and popular philosophers, the supporters of those causes which have just caught the public fancy or are just about to catch it. Some of them have their ears so close to the ground that they stumble blindly about, knocking over the occa-sional young architect or town planner who has briefly got himself too far forward in the parade and is wandering about in confusion.

The drum corps moves on. Directly behind it come the Militant Housewives, uniformed and aproned, marching in good order four abreast and dressed from the right, each with her child strapped to her back, papoose-fashion. They espouse a host of causes all mildly popular, most of them remarkably similar to those emblazoned upon the placards carried by the nuts and goof-balls who passed this way ahead of them. The Militant House-wives do not carry banners, for they are heavily laden with thick briefs, committee reports, studies, polls, texts on parliamentary procedure, and minutes of the last meeting.

The parade by this time has become a more stately affair. The crowd which has been laughing at the clowns and jeering at the artists and whistling at the scriveners and doffing its hat to the housewives assumes a more respectful mien. The parade is now a procession, winding its solemn way through the streets to the silent admiration of the onlookers.

Here are the lawyers – the young barristers in the forefront, the Q.C.'s well behind – suitably gowned and scrolled. Behind the lawyers march the entrenched labour leaders and behind them, brows furrowed, eyes watery behind heavy lenses and bearing the knapsacks of Heavy Responsibility on their shoulders, the major editorial writers. The editorial writers do not have to have their ears to the ground; they simply listen to the dronings of the Q.C.'s and to the judges and bishops who march along behind them. In this way they know what their position on any given subject will be.

Now there is a break in the procession and a burst of gaiety which brings a spontaneous cheer from the crowd. It is a float, bedecked with flowers and surmounted by a steam calliope playing nostalgic tunes from another century. Standing on the float, gazing resolutely forward toward the head of the parade like living statues, are the publishers and editors-in-chief. This *tableau vivant* is a crowd pleaser as is the float's message: FREEDOM OF THE PRESS, rendered in snapdragons and Easter lilies. Big businessmen, neatly pinstriped, gambol about the float like outriders distributing comfits and fortune cookies to the crowd.

Now there is a long gap in the parade and the onlookers grow restless. Will the next section never appear? The clowns have long gone by, the sound of the drums is distant, even the notes of the steam calliope are dying away. But where is the dramatic climax?

Then, hesitantly, around the corner, come a few of the bolder back benchers, their pockets stuffed with prepared speeches, mingling with the more radical members of the Opposition. The entrenched politicians, are further behind, straggling along, trying desperately but ineffectually to keep up.

There is another gap. Will the parade never end? The crowd,

no longer amused, stimulated, or even impressed, is merely bored. Suddenly there is a flourish of trumpets and a military band is seen, heralding the climax of the March of Progress. Everyone cranes his neck for a sight of the Party in Power, marching as a single unit with the Cabinet and the Prime Minister at its core. The lawmakers are carrying banners, too, beautifully decorated, and on these banners in gothic letters there is some hint of the progressive legislation that has been or is about to be or may someday (if campaign promises are fulfilled) be placed on the statute books: SUNDAY STREETCARS . . . ABOLISH CAPITAL PUNISH-MENT . . . WIDEN DIVORCE LAWS . . . FREE EDUCATION FOR ALL . . . GUARANTEED ANNUAL WAGE. . . .